THE WAUCHULA WOODS ACCORD

Toward a New Understanding of Animals

CHARLES SIEBERT

Scribner

New York   London   Toronto   Sydney

SCRIBNER
A Division of Simon & Schuster, Inc.
1230 Avenue of the Americas
New York, NY 10020

First Scribner hardcover edition June 2009

SCRIBNER and design are registered trademarks of
The Gale Group, Inc., used under license
by Simon & Schuster, Inc., the publisher of this work.

For information about special discounts for bulk purchases,
please contact Simon & Schuster Special Sales:
1-866-506-1949 or business@simonandschuster.com

The Simon & Schuster Speakers Bureau can bring authors to
your live event. For more information or to book an event,
contact the Simon & Schuster Speakers Bureau at 1-866-248-3049
or visit our website at www.simonspeakers.com.

DESIGNED BY KYOKO WATANABE
Text set in Bembo

Manufactured in the United States of America

1   3   5   7   9   10   8   6   4   2

Library of Congress Control Number: 2008041643

ISBN: 978-0-7432-9587-1

Portions of this book originally appeared in different form in
The New York Times Magazine.

Photograph credits: p. 16, courtesy of Patti Ragan; pp. 50, 52, courtesy of the
Cambridge University Press; p. 59, courtesy of Science and Behavior Books, Inc.;
p. 64, courtesy of the MIT Collection; p. 84, courtesy of the Law Exchange;
p. 88, courtesy of Wikipedia; and p. 123, courtesy of Janis Carter.

For Bex

In memory of my sister,
Marion Siebert

It so happens I'm tired of just being a man. . . .
It so happens I'm fed up—with my feet and my fingernails
And my hair and my shadow.
Being a man leaves me cold: that's how it is.

—Pablo Neruda

Ah, whom can we use then?
Not angels, not men, and the shrewd animals
Notice that we're not very much at home
In the world we've expounded.

—Rainer Maria Rilke

THE
WAUCHULA WOODS
ACCORD

Sunday. April 13, 3:24 A.M. Tonight again, wild screams woke me. Somebody's bad dream, perhaps. Or a snake that got into one of the enclosures. Or a fox. Or a bat. Sometimes all it takes to set things off around this place is a cockroach—the huge flying ones they have down here in Florida with the shiny, mahogany wings. And then it starts: those first, hollow, belly-borne chimpanzee whoops that build, faster and higher, until finally morphing into animate, ear-drum-ripping banshees on the air, the cries reverberating long afterward against the top-most metal rafters of this odd little forest's caged canopy.

This is a place built to house and heal bad dreams. A week now since I moved in here at the Center for Great Apes on the outskirts of Wauchula, in south-central Florida, and nearly every night the same hair-trigger, primal alarms have sounded, a quick lift of my bedroom's window curtains revealing yet another writhing jigsaw of furry silhouettes in the barred, upper tree boughs.

Unable to get back to sleep, I went out to sit for a while on my cottage's screened-in back porch, its old wooden ceiling fan creakily whirring overhead, stirring up at once the already tor-pid air of these mid-April nights and—with the residual hoots and grunts of my still restive neighbors—the deeply pleasant illusion that I was someplace else. That I was off in a jungle wilderness somewhere far away and long ago. Or at least at some time other than this present one of fully found wildernesses and horizons book-ended by retirement homes for former ape entertainers.

There are a number of these sorts of places now. The fast-dwindling days of our dominion have somehow come to this—the last vestiges of our own primal ancestry living where we humans have, in a sense, been trying to get the wilderness and its inhabitants all along: right next door to us. Into more familiar, more established quarters.

Still, not all ape retirement homes are alike. Just last year, in fact, I managed to gain an audience with none other than Cheeta, star of the early Tarzan movies from the 1930s and '40s, out at his retirement facility in Palm Springs, California. Said by some to be age seventy-six now, the oldest known living nonhuman primate on earth, he spends his days there riding around in a golf cart, watching tapes of his old movies on TV, banging out tunes on an upright piano, and, whenever the mood strikes him, painting: brightly swirling canvases that have been dubbed "apestract art" and that are now coveted cocktail party conversation pieces among the rich and the famous. Here at the Center for Great Apes, on the other hand, great pains are taken to try to restore the residents to some semblance of their former selves, an often difficult transition for creatures more accustomed to eating at movie caterers' tables than having to forage for their own food.

I sat out on my back porch for a good while tonight before deciding to come out here to be with Roger, waiting for the commotion to die down, wondering all the while which one of the retirees got spooked this time. Chipper, perhaps, a very popular Ringling Bros. clown in his day, still strung out from years of pedaling around the circus ring on a multiseated bicycle with his longtime performing partner and now equally wired bunk-mate Butch: a tireless ham, who, at the merest hello, will imme-diately go into one of his favorite old schticks, standing up with a broad-toothed grin and thrusting his arm into the air in the classic "ta-da!" pose.

Or it might have been Sammy who set the place off, orang-utan star of the film *Dunston Checks In*. Or Jonah and Jacob, the famous chimp twin-brother tandem you may remember from the popular "trunk monkey" commercials, chimps who wrapped up their careers with a last star turn in the recent *Planet of the Apes* remake.

And then again it could have been Bam Bam, the former sweet-faced orangutan nurse Precious in the soap opera *Passions,* an ape I first happened to see just a few weeks ago, sitting up late one night in my midwestern motel room, watching an evangelical documentary about evolution in which Bam Bam was recruited to play himself failing miserably at trying to eat a proper dinner in a crowded restaurant in order to definitively disprove the "theory" that we evolved from apes.

They're all living here now, and many others—former stars of the big screen and television; of Big Top circuses and small roadside zoo attractions—and all of them with memories as long as their careers were brief. It's a little-known fact about the ape entertainers we see. Too big and strong to use much after the age of five or six, they'll live another fifty to sixty years like this, swinging among used tires and their own brains' echolalia of brash lights and human cackling; of screaming boardwalk hawkers and air-curdling carnival calliopes—the very associa-tions I fear I must be stirring up as I pass by them each morn-ing on my way out here to Roger's place.

They are keenly aware of my presence: of my oddly famil-iar otherness and its rigidly upright movements; and of the fact that it isn't any of them I'm on the way to spend my days with. Each will rush forward as I approach, staring out and spitting at me from various perches along the fringes of their airy, high-domed enclosures: the best possible halfway houses we can build for them between their ongoing captivity and rightful sky; the outer "uncaged" branches limning the farthest reaches of our attempts at restitution before deflecting our gaze back down to these attached living quarters of skylights and swinging cots and corner-mounted platform beds.

And then they'll just settle back, one by one, and watch as I turn down the narrow gravel path that leads past the infirmary, cross the small wooden footbridge at the very heart of these grounds, and set my shoulder satchel and folding chair down once more in the small clearing before Roger's outdoor enclosure.

He's always there waiting, sounding the same three hand claps that he did the first time he saw me. And then the two of us will just settle in for another day of the very thing we're doing in here now, sitting face-to-face, staring. An alignment that I think must look so ridiculous, it's little surprise that the sight of Roger and me sitting opposite one another all day long often sends the other retirees into swirling fits of screams around us.

That's why I decided to come out and be with Roger at this late hour. Long after the screaming had stopped and all the other apes in residence—the retirees and whichever keepers are on duty—had returned to their respective sleeping quarters.

So that it could be just Roger and me alone like this. Without the others peering in, wondering what we're up to. Turning their mad circles around us. Making their constant comments behind our backs.

So that it could be just Roger and me, and we might finally get to the bottom of this strange business between us.

You can learn a lot, I've found, from just daring to remain within a chimpanzee's stare. Far more than you can from a fellow human's. There lies only refractory shards, deft deflections, sought answers, facile conquests. Into a chimp's gaze you can proceed unfettered. Toward matters truly fraught. And then take up residence there for a while. In a time well before this one. Beneath the slow-whirling ceiling fan of your suddenly becalmed, simpler brain.

Time creeps but there never seems to be time enough. Nothing much appears to happen, and yet I'll be a while now trying to catch up with the events and emotions of these past days with Roger, and with the fevered conjurings of this still unfolding night.

Three twenty-nine A.M. I'm staring at Roger's huge left forefinger—the darkly creased, inordinate humanness of it—furled, not a foot away from me, around the central crossbar of his bedroom's locked steel door.

In the room right beside us, Butch and Chipper are entwined in nested blankets atop their corner-mounted platform bed, snoring away. Just behind me, a large standing metal fan is stirring up the still night air with that warm, musky milk odor of chimpanzee.

He always positions himself this way in front of me, Roger, whether we're outdoors or inside like this: nearly two hundred pounds of him—huge for a chimpanzee—moored to one slender pipe of his own confinement; his body gently rocking back and forth; his crazed hazel eyes fixed on me; his white-freckled mouth slightly agape; the fingertips of his right hand forever worrying the stunted parapet of his bottom front teeth.

I can't tell if Roger keeps that one finger there as a fulcrum for his ceaseless rocking, or if he's purposely inviting a touch from me. But then there are a lot of things I haven't been able to figure out when it comes to my partner in sleeplessness tonight.

Of the forty-two retirees at this facility, Roger is the only one who insists on living alone. Twenty-eight years old now, another former Ringling Bros. performer, born in captivity and raised all his life around human beings, he still prefers our company to that of his fellow chimps, and—for reasons that neither I nor anyone else around this place has been able to explain— my company in particular. My company a priori.

The moment Roger saw me last week, he seemed utterly convinced that we already knew each other. Actually stood and applauded. Excited but not overly fawning applause. Three loud, slow claps of his long, leathery hands. As though he'd somehow been expecting me all along. As though to say, "Oh, you. Finally. Where have you been?"

These are not just my imaginings. A number of the caregivers have commented on it, including Patti Ragan, the woman who founded this place and has allowed for my stay here. She witnessed the whole thing: the slow hand claps; the odd way Roger stood and stared out at me; the way he instantly skulked off to a far corner of his enclosure when it came time for me to tell him good-bye.

"Interesting," Ragan said as we were heading back to her house up at the front of these grounds. "He's really got something for you."

People, of course, have such notions all the time. You remind them of someone else. Or you passed them on a street one day years ago, briefly locked eyes, and then ended up regularly resurfacing, for no good reason, in their thoughts and dreams. Or you truly did figure in some prior life of theirs, one to which only they, naturally, can be privy. As for Roger, I've been able to think of any number of good reasons to discount all the above explanations, and yet somehow the least of them is the fact that he is a chimpanzee.

Three thirty-three A.M. Roger gently rocking, watching my every move; my long-lost friend and cross-species confidant ever eager, despite the late hour, for whatever might be in store tonight.

It's madness, of course, this apparent conviction of his and my indulgence of it. Inveterate ape-house lingerer that I am, nearly all the significant zoo encounters I've had with chimps would have long predated Roger.

Still, something about him does seem familiar, aside from the deep biological kinship. A certain asking look on his face, a kind of sustained simian bewilderment that I know I recognize from somewhere.

Often over the course of this past week, caught up in the spell of our extended stare-downs, I've even allowed myself the fantasy that it was, in fact, a baby Roger who appeared before me on a New York City sidewalk early one morning back in the late summer of 1979—surely the most unlikely and memorable chimp encounter of my life: a shiny silver Airstream cruiser pulling up before my Lower East Side apartment building as I sat on the front stoop, sipping coffee, the cruiser's door swooshing open, a diapered chimpanzee stepping out and gently raising his hand toward me. Even now, tumbling headlong into the mesmeric swivels of Roger's teeth-rubbing gaze, it's easy to convince myself that I'm seeing aspects of that baby chimp's face again in his present one.

And yet aside from an approximate age match (Roger, Patti Ragan told me, was born in the early winter of that same year), he would have been nowhere near New York City in the late summer of 1979, having been raised more or less from infancy by a Florida-based circus trainer and his wife, a couple who lived not very far from here.

All my memory's possible leads have come to similar dead ends. I have, as well, gone over in my mind countless times by now that initial meeting with Roger last week, trying to decipher what about it could have so captured his fancy, or set free, perhaps, some long-trapped memory of his. At times I think it isn't me at all whom he recognized so much as he did some lingering thrill or taint from the many kindred places I'd just been to prior to showing up here in the woods of Wauchula.

For weeks I'd been traveling around the country, visiting with captive chimpanzees, a kind of impromptu farewell tour of our own kidnapped and caged primal selves. Some two to three thousand chimps are currently living in the United States (to say nothing of the number of orangutans and gorillas and other primate cousins in the country), and their numbers are only growing: a decidedly topsy-turvy moment in the history of civilization when the number of captive apes is burgeoning even as their wild populations continue to dwindle.

I met chimps everywhere in the course of my sad civil safari: in research labs and roadside zoos; chimps dressed up in American flags and party caps for children's birthdays; chimps that have been injected with everything from HIV to hepatitis for drug tests; that have been strapped to high-speed centrifuges and crash sleds for space-flight and seat-belt tests; chimps in breeding compounds for making more chimps; chimps in private homes and retirement homes for former ape actors.

This place was, in truth, something of an afterthought in my tour. A brief, last-minute stop—or so I thought at the time—before beginning the long drive north back home to my wife, Bex, in Brooklyn, New York, and the life—one that often seems a remote memory to me here—that she and I live together among our fellow human beings.

I arrived in Wauchula about midafternoon, having just made the two-hour drive from Fort Pierce, on the state's eastern coast, where I'd spent the morning visiting yet another newly established chimpanzee retirement facility, known as the Save the Chimps foundation, a series of thirteen tree-dotted islands, each with its own set of jungle gyms and pastel-colored housing units: a sprawling, man-made ape archipelago within the very heart of human senescence.

A voice in the center's front-gate speaker box explained that Patti Ragan was out on the grounds, but that she would be coming to meet me shortly. Even from that vantage point, I could tell that this place was nothing like Cheeta's golden years digs: a white stucco ranch house in a neatly coiffed Palm Springs suburb, the entire right side of the home done up in a jungle safari motif, replete with bamboo lanterns; a bolted-down bronze statue of the star himself (it had been stolen once before by vandals); and a big "La Casa de Cheeta" sign on the wall of his quarter's grass-hut-styled entrance—a nod to Cheeta's famous late neighbor's place just up the block: "La Casa de Liberace."

Just beyond the center's main office headquarters and Ragan's nearby bungalow-style house loomed a dense, semitropical tangle of oak and bay trees; magnolia and sweet gums; Florida pines and huge, fan-leafed, sable palms, the whole steamy effulgence of it wreathed in the light, ethereally sweet smell of orange blossoms from the miles of surrounding groves.

Here and there through the upper tree boughs I could see the now familiar furry silhouettes, either hunched over or swinging through branches. The arcing, green-colored curves of their geodesic-dome-like enclosures melded so seamlessly with the surrounding flora, it seemed for a moment that I was about to enter some primordial primate paradise.

Just then a tan golf cart came speeding out from the brush. The driver—a short, compact woman dressed in blue jeans and a denim work shirt, her sandy brown hair pulled back in a ponytail—slammed to a gravelly stop, got out, and opened the front gate, holding in her arms a diapered, five-year-old chimp with cerebral palsy named Knuckles, still quite groggy from the anesthesia he'd been given for an MRI exam up in Gainesville.

"Sorry," Patti Ragan said, hopping back in the cart and placing Knuckles on the seat between us. "Things are a bit crazy around here today."

As we started off toward the woods, Knuckles reached toward me, a concerned Ragan explaining all the while that she does not allow outsiders such as myself physical contact with any of the residents for fear of the apes coming down with something. All the caregivers at the facility, she said, are required to get health clearances, but she was a bit short of help at the moment and more worried about leaving Knuckles unattended in his current state.

For all of my recent travels among chimpanzees, both the supplanted ones here in the States and some of the few remaining wild ones in Africa; for all of my childhood stare-downs with chimps in zoo ape houses and the attendant conviction, one that Roger has now seemingly confirmed, that I am uncommonly attuned to them and their unique brand of intelligence—this was the first time I'd been this close to a chimpanzee.

At one point, Knuckles grasped on to my hand as we drove along in Ragan's golf cart, the warm, thick casks of his palm and underfingers beginning to squeeze so tightly around my own comparatively frail ones that I thought they might suddenly burst, like a couple of hastily tied-off carnival-balloon fingers.

There was that same sweet, musky-milk chimp scent, and each time I looked down at Knuckles, I was met by his wide-smiling, swimmy-eyed gaze, a visage that, as ridiculous as this might sound, reminded me of a young Jerry Lewis playing a chimp.

I never felt at once so secure and unsteady in all my life: Knuckles clasping on to my arm while I kept inwardly feeling about for some mooring within the deep-brown, druggy swirl of his eyes. It was as though he were dreamily swinging somewhere among tree limbs even as my own kept lurching to become the arboreal ones I imagined him grasping for.

Ragan drove on, Knuckles staring upward, my vertigo suddenly deepening with thoughts of the child Bex and I had been expecting a few years earlier, only to lose it to a late miscarriage: my by now long-dormant parenting impulses reawakened by a clasping, palsied chimpanzee. Each squeeze of Knuckles' thick palms triggered the next memory from those days, down to the last dizzyingly expectant one with Bex at the birthing clinic, when a young Russian technician in tight jeans and patent-leather high heels abruptly withdrew from Bex's belly the sonogram wand that she clearly wielded more deftly than she did the English language.

"Sorry," she told us. "It is demise."

Pulling Knuckles' hand away, Ragan took me first around

the perimeter of the grounds, alternately pointing out the wild fruit trees—tangerine, grapefruit, orange, and papaya—and the considerable damage wrought by the previous year's hurricanes. She showed me some of the new enclosures currently under construction for future arrivals, and took me past the guest cottage in which I'm now staying.

She then started along the very route I take here to Roger's place each day, going from one enclosure to the next, introducing me to my future neighbors, launching into her signature, rapid-fire biographies of each one, complete with their performance records and film credits: these lifelong, languishing cast-offs of a few minutes of our laughter.

We stopped at one point in an open area far from any of the enclosures, and it wasn't until I followed Ragan's upturned gaze that I realized we were directly beneath one of the overhead walkways and the hairy red back of a skyward-gazing Bam Bam, the orangutan I'd recently seen in the evangelical anti-evolution documentary throwing around his salad and chewing on the tablecloth as the show's cohosts, a former childhood TV star named Kirk Cameron and his the Way of the Master ministry cofounder, Ray Comfort, sat smugly smiling on either side.

Eight years old now, Bam Bam has been out of the movies for some time, and yet with just his head turned toward Ragan and me in a classically insouciant orangutan greeting ("orangs," as Ragan calls them, tend to be far more laid back and solitary than chimps), he still had that same startled, baby-face visage I remembered from the documentary.

"He's a very sweet, gentle ape," Ragan said, Bam Bam's wide, knowing eyes fixed on me and Knuckles, that inescapable, multisided sadness one can't help feeling—both for the retirees and about us—beginning to overtake me.

Ragan stood in her seat and reached toward the overhead

walkway to give one of Bam Bam's protruding toes a squeeze. She then drove on toward the center of the facility. In moments we were stopping at Butch and Chipper's enclosure, directly across from Roger's, and I've often wondered since if it wasn't something about the sight of Knuckles and me in the cart that day that might have set off some particular memory from Roger's own strangely peopled past.

"Chipper is very neurotic," Ragan explained, the two of us staring at his hairy frame, suspended midway up the front bars, screaming and pounding. "He needs constant attention, and I didn't say my usual hello to him today."

Just then another chimp emerged from the far back of the same enclosure. Tall and slender, he strode upright toward us, came alongside, and sat down next to a suddenly becalmed Chipper.

"And that's Butch," Ragan said, her hand instantly shooting up to her mouth as though trying to put back the snappily absent "Hello" that had just come out of mine, Butch immediately going into one of his "ta-da!" poses, which, in turn, set off Chipper again and a number of the other retirees around us: a maelstrom of raucous chimp high jinks that were at once punctuated by a loud hand clap, like the pounding of a judge's gavel in a disorderly courtroom, followed by two more. And that's when I turned and first saw Roger.

He was pressed flush against the front of his enclosure, a particularly imposing figure in the upright position at well over five feet, his left hand holding high to the fencing above him, the fingertips of the right hand manically worrying those front teeth of his. Mostly, though, I was struck by that stare, his flaring, deep-set hazel eyes peering out at me with what, to my deep discomfort, I'd soon realize is their unchanging expression.

It is a beguiling mix of amazement and apprehension, the look, as I've often thought of it since, of a being stranded between his former self and the one we humans have long been suggesting to him. A sort of hybrid of a chimp and a person. A veritable "humanzee."

I knew right then, I suppose, that I would be staying here for a while longer. That there were a number of things Roger and I needed to get to the bottom of.

It isn't often, after all, that a chimp reminds you of a journey you'd forgotten you were even on. Not so much my recent travels both here in the States and, in the months just before that, the jungles of Uganda, although I have found that Roger's very presence has brought those memories back to me more vividly than I might ever have imagined.

But I'm referring as well to the larger, overarching venture that is anyone's life, and to the many encounters I've had over the years not just with chimpanzees but with a number of different creatures. Encounters in which I've gotten the purest glimpses into our human essence through the eyes of the sentient non-us. Encounters in which I've felt the least of that telltale skittishness that animals so readily detect in us humans precisely because I am in the company of other animals.

That, anyway, is how I tried to explain things when I first phoned Bex last week back in Brooklyn to say that I'd be extending my trip to move in with a chimpanzee. Of course, considering that I'd originally set out weeks earlier in an ultimately futile attempt to meet with an entirely different chimpanzee, named Ripley—resident of a small roadside zoo in Nebraska—this latest development with Roger seemed to Bex a kind of progress. An indication that I was perhaps settling down a bit, that I had at last found what I didn't even know I was looking for when I first left Brooklyn last month.

Do we each have in this world an extant version of our former simian selves? A primatological doppelgänger and pre-assigned escort back into our own animality?

I can't say for certain. All I know is that I'd never have posited such a thing until I met Roger.

Three thirty-eight A.M. Roger has me once more in his thrall, this web of focus that he weaves around us with each teeth-rubbing wobble of his wide-eyed gaze. One false move on my part, the slightest sign of restlessness—a shift in my seat, a wayward glance, a dozy eyelid—and he'll know it the way a spider does the merest tap on the outmost strands of its orb.

Don't waver, his wild stare seems to be commanding me. Keep venturing the wordlessness, the apparent blankness.

Outside now, the compound seems fully settled again, just the peepers and the crickets, and the occasional owl. Mounted on the wall above me, meanwhile, are two of the surveillance cameras through which Patti Ragan keeps track of all her charges at night, their lenses perusing Roger's room and Butch and Chipper's.

I shouldn't be here at this hour. If one of the caregivers were to find me; if Ragan were to notice my seated silhouette in one of the camera monitors that she has mounted in the kitchen of her house, I could lose my visiting privileges altogether. Get booted back to Brooklyn before ever learning what Roger wants, or where he thinks we could possibly know each other from.

I'm not sure what came over me tonight. It's not as if Roger and I haven't been getting enough time together by day. But something happened. Something to do, perhaps, with all the time I have spent here: the dawn of day five now living among retired ape actors. Some sort of record, I would imagine. Uncharted terrain.

How to describe it?

A daily acquiescence of the self. A steady shuffling off of my personhood in the direction of the non-me of being, and with Roger here as my personal guide. Even as he seems to be looking to me to help him in the other direction, toward his own inherent humanness: like two primates, you might say, passing in the night.

I remember in the wake of that first wave of screams tonight feeling wholly lost for a moment as to who or what I even am: a bliss of creaturely anonymity that I was all at once desperate to prolong. To continue to inhabit, before the cage of my one, brief human life span could begin to close in around me again, and force me back into being just a man.

I sat out there in the screened and wooded darkness, eyes closed, not wanting to see my hands, or my feet, or any other too-familiar, pallid part of me, waiting all the while for another squall of screams to sound. Another wave of unbridled terror upon which to keep riding away from myself. Before that relentless keeper that is human consciousness could begin to rein me back in. To close, one by one, the doors on all the other creatures I know myself to be, and to once have been, including Roger.

And it was just then, in that brief abeyance of being—when I'd yet to fully awaken to myself again and thus had one less set of bars to place between Roger and me—that I realized I should be out here with him. That after a week of daylight visits, this unlikely hour might yield something different, might be the optimum time for Roger and me to meet.

Terrible insomniac that I knew Roger to be, I figured he was awake well before the screaming started and would likely be whenever I got out here. Ragan told me that often when she gets up in the middle of the night, she'll see Roger on one of her kitchen monitors, sitting up alone in his room, staring out the small window by his bed, manically rocking.

I went back into the cottage and started packing up my shoulder satchel with Roger-vigil essentials: a notebook, pens, a tape recorder (I wasn't anticipating much in the way of vocalization at this hour, either from Roger or any of the others, but I decided to bring it along anyway), and finally some reading material: *The Metaphysics of Apes* in this case, a book the cover of which seemed to transfix Roger when he first set eyes on it the other afternoon.

I paused a moment at the cottage's front door before leaving. Then, when it seemed to be just me and the peepers and the crickets and the owls again, I slipped outside and started off in this direction, taking great care along the way not to stir up again any of my once famous neighbors. None of them with quite the star wattage of Cheeta, to be sure, but notable figures in their own right and—as unwitting outcasts of their original nature—beings far more akin to us than their biology already dictates.

I passed the orangutan Radcliffe's place, just across from mine, and Bam Bam's. Passed Mowgli, a former cohost of a number of late-night talk shows; and Oopsie, an understudy to the star of the TV show *BJ and the Bear.* I passed Jonah and Jacob, and then, to my great relief, made it without incident past a volatile quartet of young retirees: Jam, Koda, Bella, and Ellie, new arrivals here, best known for their recent parts in a number of popular careerbuilders.com commercials in which they play a group of nattily suited office workers run amok, tearing up files, bouncing off the walls and furniture, pulling down their pants and sitting on the office copy machine.

And yet once past them, it required even more stealth getting in here to Roger unnoticed. The only access to these nighttime quarters is through a small areaway beneath the center's oldest central housing unit, a place where a number of the overhead metal walkways that connect all the different high-domed ape enclosures intersect.

Think of a forest with an Erector set skeleton of skyways and platforms built into its canopy, a fixed array of assigned perches and straightened vine-swings: orangutans and chimps daily shuffling between their enclosures, or on their way to and from the infirmary for a medical checkup; or to the kitchen for some food. A metropolis-like rendering of what in the wilderness, if you've never had the thrill of witnessing it, is the fluidic and rampantly graceful core of any human city's cemented commerce.

A pair of metal doors on either side of this unit's central areaway leads to the inner sleeping quarters of whichever chimps the keepers have decided to group together. The daily mixing and matching of the center's residents is a complex geometry of its own: keepers opening and shutting the little doors built into the overhead passageways between the different enclosures to allow assigned intermingling between whichever chimps are getting along, or orangutans, but never, of course, between chimps and orangutans, the former being from Africa and the latter from Southeast Asia.

I found the areaway doors propped open tonight because of the heat, a pair of large standing metal fans on either side of the areaway keeping the humid air and chimp musk circulating as I made my way inside. I tiptoed past the sleeping Butch and Chipper, mindful the whole time of their little performance last week, then looked up and saw Roger just as Patti Ragan had described seeing him on her kitchen monitor: sitting up in bed, wide awake, staring out his small bedside window, rocking.

I moved a few steps closer and was just about to wave a hand to get Roger's attention when it occurred to me that my sudden appearance at such a strange hour might startle him, set him off into fits of screaming that would ignite the whole place again, bringing the entire night-duty staff down on me.

In an instant I lost all resolve, found myself slowly backing up toward the open areaway doors, determined now to return to the cottage and go back to bed. And I very nearly made it. Got all but my head and one air-tamping hand back into the double-scented shadow of Butch and Chipper's room when Roger turned and spotted me.

He hopped soundlessly down—it's stunning how quietly chimpanzees move their heft—then shuffled forward through his bedroom's clutter of science magazines and old Yellow Pages (Roger's favorites), sounding those same three hand claps along the way, but softly now, more or less miming them, in deference to the hour and his jumpy neighbors, even emitting a few muffled hoots of excitement as he settled in before me.

"Hello, Roger," I whispered, then carefully opened and set down the little folding chair that is left here against the wall for my indoor daytime sessions with Roger. During rainy spells mostly, when he and I will watch on my computer one of the Tarzan DVDs I originally obtained for my visit with Cheeta a year ago.

Roger looked on intently as I took a seat and opened my satchel. They miss very little, our nearest kin. One of the caregivers told me that Chipper notices when people are wearing contact lenses, sees his reflection in them, and often reaches to try to touch his own image.

I was also warned to watch what I say around any of the retirees. A couple of the keepers here were recently talking in front of a chimp named Kenya about making a little pool for her and the others to play in, and she immediately ran off to grab a plastic tub at the back of her enclosure.

Another caregiver happened to mention one morning within earshot of Grub, a former roadside-zoo chimp here, that two much-loved enrichment volunteers might be visiting the facility. Grub, who particularly enjoys painting and making cutout masks from pieces of paper and cardboard for the people he likes, quickly climbed to the highest perch in his enclosure and waited there all day for the volunteers, who never showed.

If it was a movie that Roger was expecting tonight, he gave little indication of it. Showed no signs of disappointment when I first sat down and pulled out only my field notebook. Roger will not hesitate to register his disappointment with me, especially when he senses that I'm getting ready to leave.

Roger hates it when I leave him, even if it's just to go back to the cottage to grab some lunch. Or when I decide to turn in for the day, usually long after the sun has gone down and all the other apes have retired to their quarters. The minute he sees me start to gather up my things, he'll go into his retreat-and-sulk mode, promptly standing, walking to a far corner of his enclosure, and then plunking down there with his shoulders hunched and his back turned. He'll often desert me at the merest sign of my attention beginning to drift.

He isn't, I soon realized, demanding that I pay attention to him so much as that I simply pay attention. Somehow, after a lifetime of gawking, grabby circus and roadside-zoo audiences, the very proximity of my concentrated, nonirritable presence seems to be balm enough. Roger clearly likes to be directly addressed, to be either spoken or read to, and he particularly enjoys our watching movies together. But he is also fine with us just sitting quietly together like this, easing each other out of our respective insomnias.

It is, I think, that telltale human skittishness—our inability to abide an apparent blankness—that Roger cannot, in turn, abide in me. He'll immediately get up and walk off to his corner, holding there for some time. He does eventually return, but always settling in again at a slightly askance angle, his left shoulder pressed to the bars, his head bowed and canted toward me: a posture disturbingly reminiscent of a priest awaiting a confession.

Tonight, as I've said, he seemed quite content with seeing only the notebook emerge from my satchel, and yet I still had to take care with it. Roger, you see, is also a stickler for ritual and detail, and this is a notebook he'd not seen before, one I decided to break out especially for this unique occasion. It is exactly like the red, hardcover, college-rule, journal-style notebook Roger has been watching me write in all this week, except that this one happens to be black.

I held it up first for Roger's approval. He regarded it for a moment with those slow swivels of his hazel-eyed gaze. Then he just sat and watched as I turned to the first blank page and launched into these scribblings, lines that I soon realized were, in some bizarrely perfect symbiosis, being drawn out of me by Roger's focused, nearly absorptive presence, even as the very act of writing them seemed to be further settling and soothing him.

To the point where I've now become fearful of even pausing, not wanting to disrupt the very dynamic that might finally yield whatever Roger and I are seeking from one another.

Three forty A.M. The sense now of time's complete distention: Roger still rubbing his teeth, staring at me with that ever-startled gaze. Butch and Chipper snoring away next door. The fans whirring. The night air bristling with the peepers and the crickets and, out beyond this forest's metal rafters, the ongoing stars.

I feel I'm living out that childhood fantasy of being left behind at the old city-zoo ape house after closing hours, finally allowed to pursue at my leisure all those past stare-downs that were ever arrested by a shuffling crowd or the tug of an impatient parent's hand.

Allowed to plumb with Roger every nook and nuance of this unlikely hour, when no other member of my species is around, and all the tortured machinations of our attempts to atone for past entrapments seem to weigh less heavily on my senses.

"Keep on," a strange, far-off voice intones now, as though from some inward, primeval bog of my own brain—a place where it at once thrills and terrifies me to realize both Roger and I have been before; a place where he and I were one and without words.

Three forty-three A.M. I'm still staring at his bar-poised forefinger, calculating all the possible consequences of my touching it. Scenarios ranging from the cartoonish—Roger and I melding in a barred embrace of instantly unleashed recognition and recompense—to the calamitously real: my touch instantly waking him to an uncontrollable rage, peals of his pent-up psychosis also sounding the alarm that I'm where I shouldn't be.

Along the floor in front of my chair, midway between my feet and Roger's hand, runs a painted red line. It marks the closest point that a nonofficial visitor such as myself is supposed to get to any of the enclosures. The line is there both to help guard against the retirees coming down with something and to keep someone such as me from losing a finger.

Chimps are—the cutesy, playful image that we nurture of them in their acting roles notwithstanding—wild animals, five times stronger than the strongest human, capable of making short work of a carelessly proffered hand. Roger, I feel fairly certain, would never harm me. And yet something Patti Ragan said after my initial tour last week has thus far kept me on my side of the red line.

We were having coffee up in the kitchen of her airy bungalow with its exposed wood rafters and ceiling fans, an array of tall potted trees, and an orphaned parrot in a large standing cage. Somewhere in the course of her pondering my pleas for residency here—and I was fairly shameless about it, even carrying on at one point about how much the cottage I'm now living in reminded me of the log cabin that Bex and I retreat to each summer in the woods of Canada—Ragan began telling me about the various people who pass through and sometimes spend a night here: enrichment counselors; former "parents"; people from the local community volunteering their services; schoolkids and teachers on educational tours.

Roger, I was not surprised to learn, loves it when people

visit. And yet, Ragan went on to say almost in passing, whenever Roger sees a white-haired man of a certain build—a largish man, broad-shouldered, a little over six feet, "your type of build," Ragan abruptly announced, her eyes widening—everything, she told me, but for my hair, which, fifty-two years now into this life still clings tenuously to its original shade of brown—he'll immediately go into fits of fearful screaming, banging his head against the sides of his enclosure, sitting up for hours afterward, manically rocking.

"There is something about that type of man," she said. "It just sets Roger off. We don't know what it is. Something in his past."

It is never far from my mind, whenever I'm with Roger, 3:47 A.M. now, still nothing demonstrable to report: the fact that there is literally a hairbreadth between his apparent fondness for and his deathly fear of me. The fact that he and all the other retirees have, like us, minds enough to lose and histories that can only hasten the process.

The screams that sound here at night can come from dark places. The other evening I was sitting in the little primate library that Patti Ragan has assembled in the main conference room of the facility headquarters just across from her house. I came at one point upon an account of a training session for Butch and Chipper's former Ringling Bros. act, one in which they and one other chimp pedaled around the ring on a four-seated bicycle steered by a fourth chimp, named Louie. The rehearsals took place in nearby Venice, Florida, under the direction of a longtime animal trainer named Mickey Antalek, whose apprentice, Nick Connell, happened to keep a journal of his experiences.

"The vehicle was difficult for even a human to ride under those circumstances," Connell recalled, "and Louie had a hard time of it, spilling the ensemble repeatedly. And repeatedly, he was struck with a sturdy club. The thumps could be heard outside the arena building, and the screams went farther than that. My blood boiled. I'm ashamed to say I did nothing."

Chipper was born and captured in the wild, meaning he also carries the memory of watching his mother getting shot. Wild chimp and orangutan mothers are fiercely protective of their children, and animal poachers can't be bothered with the added expense of tranquilizer guns. This same dynamic applies as well to most of the zoo and circus elephants we've ever seen, and to many of those in African wildlife parks as well. Taken as babies by poachers for the entertainment industry or by game wardens in the process of forcefully relocating wild elephant herds, the sudden orphans are often chained to the bodies of their dead parents until they can be transported to their new homes.

My second night here, Ragan stopped by the cottage to see how I was faring and to drop off some literature about the current plight of wild orangutans, among our closest primate relatives after chimps. Ragan told me that she has a special feeling for the "orangs." After closing her prosperous Miami-based temp service, she opened this place in the wake of a trip she'd made to Southeast Asia, where she encountered her first orangutans in the wild.

The steady encroachment and habitat destruction that have long been marginalizing apes and elephants and countless other of the world's large land-based animals is now occurring in a kind of dizzying hyperspeed throughout the orangutans' natural range, largely as a result of the expanding international market for palm oil.

A core ingredient of thousands of household products sold primarily in Europe, India, and China—everything from ice cream and cookies to soap, toothpaste, and laundry detergent—palm oil is now being harvested on vast plantations throughout Borneo and Malaysia, destroying in the process millions of acres of rain forest and the animals indigenous to them, including an estimated five thousand orangutans annually, a rate that will eliminate the species within the next ten years.

In some of the pamphlets Ragan brought that night there were images of orangutans whose heads and hands had been chopped off as trophies by loggers and plantation workers; orangutans that had been buried alive up to their necks to be slowly tortured; others doused in fuel and set alight. There was one photo of an adult female orangutan who'd been fully shaved and then chained for weeks to the bed of one of the plantation workers' huts as a sex slave.

They often have, I've come to notice, a distinctive timbre of their own, orangutan screams. Just as loud as those of the chimps, but more high-pitched; "bare-teethed screams," they're called, like the frayed, frantic appeals of a frightened newborn, cries that become increasingly hoarse and then eventually trail off into a strangled, choking sound.

I sat out on the back porch that night after Ragan left, thinking about all these dire dispatches we keep hearing from the world's last wilderness frontiers: the imminent loss of apes and large cats; the whole-scale collapse of elephant culture that I'd just gone to Africa to report on; polar bears clinging with spindrift gazes to the planet's last, fast-dwindling ice floes; even the world's once seemingly limitless oceans being rendered outsized, madness-inducing echo chambers: reports now coming in from all over the globe of beached whales and dolphins dying in agony from the bends, having surfaced too quickly to escape the new high-tech sonar of naval and fishing vessels.

On and on it goes, the wildlife endgame you never thought possible in your own lifetime. As I sat staring out through the back porch screen at the pale glints of moonlight along this forest's uppermost rafters, Bam Bam and Knuckles and Roger and the rest of them here suddenly seemed to me the safe, the anointed ones. Passengers in a prototype for some huge super-Ark in which we will soon be taking with us whichever animals we ultimately decide to save from the irrepressible tide of ourselves.

Three fifty A.M. now. Roger has stopped the teeth-rubbing for a moment, his fingertips just resting atop his lower lip, his eyes still fixed on me but with a softer, distracted air, as though he's briefly lost in thought.

I do know something of his past. Born at a Florida roadside zoo in the winter of 1979, he was sold to a Florida-based circus trainer who groomed Roger for his career at Ringling Bros., a process that included castration. He would go on to play the cello for the next ten years in an all-chimp orchestra, one of Ringling Bros.' most popular acts.

The trainer and his wife kept Roger in a cage in the family garage alongside another chimp, Sally, Roger's one and only close chimp companion over the course of his life. After Sally died and the trainer was forced to retire due to illness, his wife decided to dispatch Roger to a small roadside zoo in nearby Kissimmee, Florida, called Jungle Land.

The wife had originally considered sending Roger here, but knowing how much Roger liked people, she felt he would get more contact with them at a place such as Jungle Land. He wound up in a narrow, shadeless pen there—Ragan showed me some pictures of it—alongside Radcliffe, the former circus orangutan who now lives just across the way from my cottage.

Roger, it seems, was terrified of the much larger Radcliffe at Jungle Land, the two of them separated by only a chain-link fence. One day, Radcliffe actually started breaking through the fence. A local vet was called and got there just in time to knock Radcliffe down with tranquilizers. Shortly afterward, Ragan petitioned the owners of Jungle Land to give her custody of both apes, and in the late fall of 2002, the two of them were brought here.

Ragan has made repeated attempts since then to socialize Roger with the other retirees, trying any number of different combinations in hopes of something clicking between him and at least one other chimp. Her most recent efforts have involved pairing Roger with a thirty-seven-year-old female chimpanzee here named Denyse. A former pet who spent the first thirty-five years of her life in a suburban household, knowing only human beings and eating our food, Denyse seemed an ideal partner for Roger, but thus far all attempts at pairing them have only ended in fracases and hurt feelings.

None of this, however, gets me any closer to the identity of that white-haired man. It could be anyone. Roger's deranged version of Radcliffe, perhaps; or some menacing Jungle Land visitor whom Roger encountered one day; or a half-dressed Ringling Bros. clown he happened to see backstage once as a young chimp after a show; or just a drunken friend of Roger's trainer, someone who quietly slipped into the family garage one night in the midst of a wild party and taunted Roger and Sally with booze and a lit cigarette.

He could, in the end, be just a figment from one of Roger's bad dreams. And then again, he could be me. Or the person Roger subliminally believes I am. A person he won't fully recognize, perhaps, until I touch his hand. As if Roger made up his mind from that very first moment he saw me last week that I am, in fact, the white-haired man, and this seeming rapport of ours has been nothing more than an elaborate trap Roger has laid to exact a long-awaited revenge. A trap the very bait for which has been that bar-poised finger of his.

I'll reach over to take it, and he'll quickly take hold of me.

Gently at first, and then with the sudden resurgence of a ruined wildness and five times my strength, my whole arm, through the bars, and then my shoulder and head. Enough of me, in the end, to leave my life entirely up to him.

"Go on," that inner bog voice intones, and I see a hand, as though not my own, beginning to move through the air beyond the red line. Tapping at the very edges of that tensile web Roger has woven between us, just waiting for him to fully awake to who I am and then take me in, his warm, musky scent melding now with the rusty essence of my own spilled blood, and that inner voice still droning, "Go on . . . and on . . . it's a fine way to die."

And yet he never seems to want anything more from me than my company, my vigilance, as though that alone is some unseen hand, soothing him and his long-embattled psyche.

It is, they say, a corrupted communion, this one between a captive creature and its captor, and I've known it the other way around. Those charged encounters rapidly fading from the collective human experience, like so many dislodged stars from a clear night sky, when it is just you and a wild predator alone on its terms.

The jaguar I'd been tracking one morning years ago in the jungles of Belize when it suddenly doubled back on my trail, coming up soundlessly behind me merely for one extended, coolly assessing stare before turning and padding back off into the brush.

Or the elephant matriarch I encountered in Uganda's Queen Elizabeth National Park just a few months ago, holding me fast in my tracks with a fierce widening of a tusk-white eye as her calf foraged about beneath her within the secure cribbing of four massive legs.

Or the entire pod of wild chimpanzees I would come upon

after hours of tracking through the Ugandan rain forest. At least thirty of them lounging high above in a cageless canopy, and the image, etched now forever in my brain, of one little baby's head popping out over the edge of its treetop nest for a long peek down at me.

And yet it was, I realize now, in part because of that last memory that I decided to move in here with Roger for a while. Because even as he first clapped those hands last week and fixed me with that gaze of his, I recalled myself dashing through the jungle after the phantom hoots and screams of those wild chimps and their fleet movements through the brush, and it occurred to me that Roger had never had a like experience.

That in Roger we humans have created a complete evolutionary anomaly: a chimpanzee with a name and yet no recollection of a tree.

Who or what then is Roger? That, as absurd as it may sound, is the question I often feel he is asking me. Is the very reason he clapped his hands that first day and finally called a meeting with one of his own makers, one with whom he clearly feels some special affinity.

As though he truly does recognize me. If not in the immediate sense of our having actually crossed paths somewhere before, then as a sort of kindred spirit in an equally discomfited frame. Just another out-of-sorts ape actor, you might say. One who has yet to retire from or ever feel quite comfortable in the role of being human.

I'll never know what it is like to have Roger's brain. Still, I think he knows that in me there's some semblance of himself sitting on the far side of his enclosure. That he and I were once—and not very long ago—one and the same being.

The billions of years of biology that he and I share, the common ancestry—all of that is assumed between Roger and me, intuited, felt. Somehow it's the microscopically brief blips of our respective lifetimes on this earth and of the divergent evolutionary paths that formed our different brains that we both sense hold the larger, timeless mystery.

Shortly before setting off last month on the journey that

would ultimately lead me here to Roger, I found myself late one New York City winter afternoon standing in a giant walk-in cooler filled with different animal brains. They were set on metal shelves all around me, adrift in glass containers of formaldehyde, a ghostly constellation of coiled cerebrum: gorilla and orangutan brains; rhesus macaque, spider monkey, moose, and bat brains.

On a smaller set of shelves at the back of the cooler was an array of seabound brains: octopus, porpoise, dolphin, killer whale. Directly below them, at the base of a huge Rubbermaid garbage container, was a sperm whale brain, like the one with which Moby Dick outwitted Captain Ahab: a huge, fleshy, white disk about the circumference of a café table.

Along the shelves opposite the monkey and gorilla brains was an assortment of human ones: all the mass and mindfulness that these variously sized cranial engines had once powered gone now; life paired down to a pale, multitiered assortment of inert nubs.

"And this," Dr. Patrick Hof said to me, reaching back among the gorilla and orangutan specimens for the brain I had asked him to show me, "is the chimpanzee."

I'd gone to see Hof, a neuroscientist at the Mount Sinai School of Medicine in upper Manhattan, in anticipation of my meeting with Ripley, the roadside zoo chimpanzee in Nebraska I had originally set out from Brooklyn last month to find.

I had in mind at the time writing some sort of book about chimpanzees. Not about them in the wild so much as telling the more recent and, somewhat paradoxically, less familiar tale of them in civilization; on our turf and terms; a tale that the story of Ripley's life and times seemed to me to perfectly encapsulate.

A former chimp entertainer like Roger, Ripley was to become one of the first resident retirees of the Carson Center for Chimps—as in Johnny Carson, the late, great king of late-night TV—a onetime state-of-the-art primate containment facility originally funded by the famed talk-show host and built on the grounds of a small roadside animal attraction known as Zoo Nebraska, situated just outside the town of Royal in the heart of Antelope County, about an hour and a half's drive northwest of Carson's hometown of Norfolk, Nebraska.

Early one September Saturday in 2005, a Zoo Nebraska worker, according to a newspaper report of the incident, failed to adequately secure the lock to the outdoor chimp enclosure at the Carson Center after his morning cleaning chores. A short time later, the center's four residents—Reuben, Jimmy Joe, Tyler, and Ripley—let themselves out.

As the chimps began dashing around the grounds in a frenzy of newfound freedom, the patrons on hand that day were forced to seek cover in the Zoo Nebraska visitors' center. Ripley and one of the other chimps were reported to have made their way into downtown Royal for a time, running through the streets, chasing one frightened teenager back into his house. Ripley then tried to enter the station house of the town's one gas depot. Upon finding the door locked, he went across the road, climbed to the top of a huge cottonwood tree in the front yard of the house opposite the station, took one long look at his surroundings, then climbed down and raced with his companion back to Zoo Nebraska.

The State Police and the Antelope County Sheriff's Department had arrived on the scene by then. A tranquilizer gun was used, but it seemed to have had no effect, and when a couple of the chimps attempted, for whatever reason, to get inside the visitors' center, the zoo's director grabbed one of the deputy sheriff's service revolvers and began shooting. Reuben, Jimmy Joe, and Tyler were all killed. Ripley managed in the midst of the chaos to get back to the Carson Center and through the still-open door of his enclosure.

Often in the months following the Zoo Nebraska breakout, I'd find myself sitting up in the siren-laced teem and thrum of a Brooklyn night, thinking about Ripley, all by himself out there at the Carson Center, surrounded by nothing but cornfields and wind: a lone chimpanzee clinging to the bars of his own displacement smack in the middle of a country still denying its kinship with him. What, I kept wondering, goes through such a creature's mind, one we now know to be, in many ways, as mindful as our own.

The specimen that Dr. Hof was holding before me in his cooler that afternoon looked exactly like the human brains on the shelves just over my shoulder, but in miniature, roughly half the size, like a scaled-down, working model for ours. Or, as Dr. Hof described it to me at one point, "about the size of a child's brain before puberty," a description that would come to mind often in the course of my subsequent travels among chimpanzees, now said to have the sentience of a human five-year-old: like ongoing, superannuated children.

Dr. Hof studies all kinds of animal brains to better understand the ways by which ours come undone with age, succumbing to the cognitive dismantling of diseases such as dementia and Alzheimer's and cancer. Along the way, however, he's also learned a lot about the brain of our nearest kin, uncovering a number of clues as to just how far along the same evolutionary path as our own the chimp's brain actually came. Or to put it another way, just how little a distance it is, in the end, that Roger and I have to travel now to reach one another.

Time was, and not so long ago, when the varied lights emanating from the now dead stars in Dr. Hof's cooler seemed as disparate and unknowable to us as those in the night sky once did to early humans, the stuff of science's first story: myth. In the story now being written, however, there isn't a brain we can look at that doesn't reveal to us something about the greater neuronal nebulae of which our and all brains are at once composed and a part.

There weren't, as far as I knew, any cockroach brains on Dr. Hof's shelves that day. Yet much of what we've come to know about the primordial origins and makeup of our and all brains can be traced to the tiny speck of fatty white tissue that, some ten years ago, I watched a neuroscientist in his lab in Old Westbury, Long Island, scoop from the head of a South American cockroach, a creature very much like the mahogany-winged ones that can set this place off at night: nearly two inches long and similarly disposed to flight, but with a lighter, walnut coloring.

The particular roach brain I was looking at that day in Old Westbury belonged to one of hundreds of South American roaches being kept there, all of them distant descendants of one original group of stowaway roaches that first arrived in the United States back in 1939 in a crate of Amazonian monkeys delivered to the biology department of Rockefeller University in New York City.

The monkeys were intended for the lab of Dr. Ernst Scharrer, a young German biologist who, a few years earlier as a graduate student at the University of Munich, had discovered something startling in the brains of fish, something no one had ever thought possible before about any brain: that their neurons secreted blood-borne chemicals, like all other bodily organs or glands.

Ernst would soon set about trying to confirm this same function, now known as "neurosecretion," in other vertebrates. Berta, his wife, a fellow biology student at the University of Munich and an expert on honeybee brains, decided to turn the focus of her search for neurosecretion on the backboneless world of insects, a decision prompted in large part by necessity: women scientists rarely got research positions in those days, to say nothing of the funding to afford lab monkeys.

Thus, when Berta saw the South American roaches come scurrying out of her husband's monkey crates, one of science's most unlikely and fruitful lifetime lab tandems was born. By the time she'd retired at age eighty-eight and bequeathed her roach collection to the lab at Old Westbury, Scharrer had divined within the cockroach brain the very foundations of our own sympathetic nervous system: the ways in which our brains literally body our lives forth, shaping everything from our early growth and development in the womb, to the ways in which our shifting emotions and psychological states affect the vigor of our immune systems, to the manner in which our bodies shut down when we die.

It would, appropriately enough, take the brain of the reviled cockroach to wholly undermine that long-standing pillar of Western thinking, the so-called mind-body schism: the illusion that our brain is a thing apart from flesh and all the billions of years of biology that it took to even arrive at that tiny white speck of tissue in a cockroach's head, to say nothing of the densely coiled reticulum within Roger's skull or within our own.

It is an illusion that—the longer I stare into the charged light behind Roger's eyes tonight—I'm coming to think is not only the reason why he is over there on his side of these bars and me on mine, but also why we humans are, in many ways, by far the more imprisoned species.

Dr. Hof was examining chimp brain tissue in his lab one day when he came upon a particularly dense concentration of oddly shaped, highly specialized neurons known as spindle cells. Often referred to as "the cells that make us human," spindle cells are rooted in our brain's more recently evolved right frontal cortex, in what might be called the source of our "over-mind," the region that, in a sense, allows the brain to regard its own functions and that engenders our self-awareness—that sense of ourselves as distinct individuals moving through the world, responding physically and emotionally to all around us.

In recent imaging tests, spindle cells have been shown to light up in our skulls like summer evening fireflies in response to a variety of different emotional and social stimuli: the picture of a loved one; scenes of others suffering; feelings of personal embarrassment, or guilt, or self-consciousness.

And yet as integral as these specialized neuronal cells seem to be to our very identity as human beings, they aren't even present in our brains at birth. They only begin to emerge, Dr. Hof explained, at about the fourth month of life and, over the course of the next four years or so, continue to grow and migrate toward their permanent home in the right frontal cortex, weaving themselves into place there in direct concert with our newly emerging sense of self—our feelings of devotion, compassion, and remorse; our sense of right and wrong: the early fabric, in effect, from which we each go on to weave our own individuality and personal life story.

The very name "spindle cells," Dr. Hof told me, derives from their resemblance to the elongated, bulbous rods, tapered at each end, upon which thread is spun, and the moment he said it I was reminded of an evening years ago up at the old log cabin that Bex and I retreat to each summer in the woods of Canada, just over the Vermont border in Quebec.

I was walking along the half-mile field path that leads from the cabin to the small work shed I've built on a far corner of the land. It was early September 2001. My mother was on the phone from New York. A widow of twenty years, my father having died of heart failure at age fifty-nine, she was trying to describe to me what it felt like to be dying now herself. To be dying in the particular manner that she was, her lung cancer having spread to her brain, and how she first sensed this.

She told me she had been standing in the shower one recent morning when she almost fell over. "It was like," she said, "someone had suddenly taken hold of a tightly wound thread in my brain and started pulling it out, unraveling it."

Dr. Hof has since found spindle cells in a number of the other mammal brains in his cooler. Along with chimps, he's found them in varying measures in the frontal cortex of all our other fellow primates. He has found them in the dolphin's brain, and in the whale's, who evolved theirs millions of years before primates did. Dr. Hof told me he was soon expecting to find spindle cells in the elephant's brain as well, suggesting, among other things, that those other animal cultures we're now dismantling both on this earth and under the sea are far more storied than we ever imagined.

As for chimps, they have not only been found to have the highest proportion of spindle cells after us, they also possess their full allotment of those cells at birth. Hof told me that this is probably because young chimpanzees become independent far sooner than human children do and have to be ready to perform tasks on their own much earlier than our offspring do.

And yet Dr. Hof also was surprised to discover that chimps can't develop brain diseases such as Alzheimer's, and neither can they die in the manner that my mother described. They can't for the simple reason that their brains don't have the sheer abundance of those highly specialized, more recently evolved neurons, such as spindle cells, that our brains have: a far more elaborately detailed and yet invariably more delicate neuronal tapestry, given at once to greater flourishes and easier fraying.

What is most recently and highly evolved in us, in other words, is what is most apt to devolve; and even our boldest creations—from towering cities, to soaring symphonies, to this strange little Erector set forest in which Roger and I are sitting tonight—are, in the end, the inspired simulacra of our own brain's exquisitely fleeting superstructure. A brain with such an expansive cognitive reach it is able to regard—much in the same way that it does the bristling fabric of a clear night sky—both its own nearly timeless beginnings and, with each suddenly dislodged star, its own inevitable unraveling over time.

I asked Dr. Hof at one point why our brains got this greater measure of overmind. He spoke about a kind of craniological Big Bang, a great neuronal explosion that occurred in the human brain some six million years ago as a direct consequence of our own particular ape ancestor's—there having been many kindred lineages that didn't survive—emergent ability to walk upright along the earth and thus literally introduce their brains to new places and challenges. To seek out different, more habitable environments and form the kinds of social groupings that at once greatly improved the survival rate of our offspring and required the expansion and refinement of our social awareness and communication skills, the capacity for cooperation, compassion, and the expression of ever more complex thoughts and emotions. Dr. Hof, in fact, thinks spindle cells probably had a vital role in the early development of language, all new imperatives to which our brain responded by weaving ever more threads around its own original spindle.

Increased socialization, it turns out, spawns ever more synapses. Culture crafts cranium. A dynamic now being recognized in varying measures in different brains across species, from crows and parrots to dolphins and whales to elephants and, of course, to our fellow primates.

Three fifty-five A.M. From the far side of the compound now, I can hear a few more muffled, bellyborne chimp whoops, as though in sleepy mimicry of the outer forest's hooting owls. Butch and Chipper are still snoring away next door. Roger continues to hold to his bedroom door's central crossbar, that wide-eyed stare of his inviting me—with each teeth-rubbing head swivel—farther and farther away from myself.

Sometimes I wish Roger would be the one to venture across this painted red line between us, that he would reach over at this very moment with that bar-poised hand of his, take hold of that thread my mother described, and pull it slowly out of my brain.

Pull it just long and far enough for me to arrive back at that not-so-distant point in evolutionary time before our ancestors began the walk that Roger's never took with us. That point when Roger and I were, in fact, still one and the same, so that I might finally see, however briefly, what he is seeing now as he looks out at me.

All that distinguishes us, I often want to tell my disturbed primate confessor, is the elaborateness of that illusion evinced by the human brain's more recently spun neuronal threads; an illusion at once so convincing and yet inherently frail that we still feel compelled to kidnap and place a good part of ourselves behind bars to bolster it.

Who or what then are we? That is the question Roger's very presence seems to be posing: hunched over there now in the shadows of his room's far corner, his back turned to me.

How did this happen? What was my betrayal this time?

Four oh-five A.M. A while since my last entry, but just a moment ago, it seems, we had each other's complete attention: exacting, inescapable, an unseen enclosure of its own; a chrysalis of concentration.

Perhaps Roger hypnotized me with those teeth-rubbing head wobbles of his. I do remember my writing hand beginning to tire. Confident by then that I'd learned enough about the nuances of Roger's temperament and the parameters of his patience, I closed the notebook, reached down into my satchel for my copy of *The Metaphysics of Apes,* and began to read, all of which Roger watched with keen interest.

Of the many books I've read in front of him in recent days, *The Metaphysics of Apes* has most captured his fancy. Written by Raymond Corbey, a lecturer at the Department of Philosophy at Tilburg University in the Netherlands, the book explores the collective impact of the relatively recent discovery—for the Western world at least—of ambiguously humanlike great apes such as Roger: "the first anthropological-cum-epistemological

analysis," to quote the jacket copy, "of the burgeoning anthro-
pological disciplines . . . their unwilling retreat from the notion
of human unicity, and from the relentless policing of the animal-
human boundary."

Roger, for his part, likes the cover: an image of a bonobo, or
pygmy chimpanzee, "dashing tri-pedally" against a ghostly white
backdrop, his left hand clutching what looks to be a scrolled
parchment, as though he's on his way to some skyborne, simian
graduation ceremony.

Roger and I were sitting outside when he first saw the image,
sunlight and rain clouds doing a protracted do-si-do for much
of that afternoon, keeping us from getting into a good rhythm.
Three or four times, a light shower would have me packing up
my bag, Roger, as usual, waiting for me to stand before he did,

the two of us about to take our respective routes inside here for cover, only to have the sun regain the upper hand.

Up and down we went. I remember at one point looking around to see a number of the other retirees in their surrounding enclosures miming our every move, staring in bewilderment at me and Roger, as though they were all taking their cues from us now: the reclusive chimp snob and his oddly gaited cohort; the two apes who do nothing all day but sit around and stare at one another.

When we were able to finally settle in for a stretch, I took out the *The Metaphysics of Apes*—the first time I had done so in front of Roger—and started flipping toward page thirty-eight of the text to look again at an image that had arrested my attention in the same way that the scroll-wielding bonobo would Roger's. An engraving done in 1641 by Nicolaes Tulp, the renowned Dutch physician and anatomist portrayed in Rembrandt's famous painting *The Anatomy Lesson,* it purports to be a portrait of a chimpanzee that had recently arrived in The Hague aboard a Dutch merchant ship returning from a trading expedition to Angola. It is believed to be the first live chimpanzee ever brought to Europe's shores.

The chimp was promptly dispatched to the private menagerie of Holland's then ruler, Stadhouder Frederick Henry, Prince of Orange. And it was there that Dr. Tulp—one of the leading figures of the Enlightenment, with its emerging emphasis on objective scientific observation and realistic representation—would sit before his subject, day after day, and proceed to compose one of the more surreal depictions of a chimpanzee imaginable.

The creature—seated atop a boulder with its mostly hairless torso and limbs, tapered elfin hands and feet, and sweetly smiling face—looks more like a potbellied forest nymph dreamily sleeping off a good drunk. Not a chimpanzee so much as an

ape-human hybrid, and one that, I suddenly realized as I sat with Roger the other afternoon, could be thought of as an uncannily apt figurative portrait of him. Of what we have, in effect, made of Roger.

I never did, however, get to the Tulp engraving that day. I was thumbing my way through *The Metaphysics of Apes* when I soon felt a palpable press on the air between Roger and me and looked up to see him with his nose pushed between the bars of his enclosure, his head craning to get a better fix on that scroll-wielding bonobo on the book's front cover, the very same way that Roger had responded the previous day to one particular scene in *Tarzan's New York Adventure* when Cheeta first steps out of a New York City taxicab, standing alone in the middle of the sidewalk, dreamily staring up at the surrounding buildings.

Chimps, I've learned, have very specific responses to visual stimuli, responses that are often based, like our own, on both their individual temperaments and personal experiences.

In the course of my recent Stateside safari, I visited a place known as Chimp Haven, a brand-new, state-of-the-art, federally funded retirement home for former research lab chimpanzees just outside Shreveport, Louisiana. A Chimp Haven entertainment counselor there showed me at one point into one of the facility's special storage rooms. It was filled with enrichment devices, everything from children's toys to rows of TV sets, VCRs, DVDs, and CD players. When I asked the counselor about the clear plastic covering on all the electronic equipment, she explained that chimps have very immediate likes and dislikes and few inhibitions about expressing them.

Observational data to date, she told me, have revealed that chimps find nature-sound CDs soothing. Younger chimps prefer kids' movies, Disney specials, *Barney*, and the like. The mature chimps' tastes, on the other hand, tend more toward melodrama and anything with lots of action and aggression. Soap operas such as *Passions* (Bam Bam's former star vehicle) and *General Hospital* are big hits, the latter, it seems, because research lab chimps have gotten so used to people in white coats. *The Jerry Springer Show* and NFL football games also are quite popular. Golf, baseball, and PBS programming (except, of course, for nature shows) are not.

And yet chimps will respond just as intensely to a static image—a photograph, or a book's cover—something I had only discovered at the very start of my journey toward Ripley last month, sitting up reading late at night in my motel room in Sioux City, Iowa, the nearest major metropolis to Royal and Zoo Nebraska.

I arrived that night deeply drained, having driven the previous day from Brooklyn straight through to Chicago, and then the following day straight to Sioux City. There was no need to knock off such big chunks of the journey like that. Ripley certainly wasn't going anywhere.

But somewhere in the course of the drive's opening hours and that initial rush one gets from just unshouldering the city and lighting out into open country, I'd made up my mind that I was going to get to Ripley as fast as possible, as though his very life and whatever might be left of his sanity depended on it. As though I were on the cusp not merely of visiting with Ripley, but also of trying to spring him—secretly loading him one night into the back of my car and then spiriting him away to some facility more like this one.

I made it to Sioux City by about 9:00 P.M., grabbed some dinner at a downtown barbecue joint, and then checked into a motel. Sleep, however, suddenly seemed as elusive to me as it does here each night to Roger. Exhausted as I was, all the miles I had put behind me, along with my growing apprehensions about what might still lie ahead with Ripley, had rendered me a thrumming tuning fork of a man.

I remember calling Bex back in Brooklyn—as much to regain my psychic bearings as to let her know my actual ones. And then I told her good night, hung up the receiver, and promptly subverted whatever inner equilibrium our conversation had restored by choosing for that night's reading an obscure, long-out-of-print work I'd managed to obtain just before leaving home.

Titled *Lucy: Growing Up Human: A Chimpanzee Daughter in a Psychotherapist's Family,* it is the singularly bizarre memoir that Dr. Maurice Temerlin, a University of Oklahoma psychology professor who died in 1988, wrote in 1975 about the experience of trying to raise a baby female chimpanzee with his wife, Jane.

People—often couples who don't have children of their own—try this with chimpanzees all the time. The Temerlins, however, already had a son and, both being psychologists, were approaching their endeavor as a serious psycho-anthropological experiment: an attempt to raise a chimpanzee entirely as a human being. To purposefully craft—in manner if not inner biological makeup—a more complete and convincing version of the "humanzee" that Roger has inadvertently become.

At least two known similar attempts had been made by psychologists prior to the Temerlins'. In the early 1900s, the Kelloggs, another husband-and-wife psychologist team, began raising a chimp named Gua along with their infant son, Donald, but abandoned the experiment after a year for reasons unknown. In the 1940s, yet another psychologist couple, the Hayeses, brought up an infant female chimp named Viki, but she died at age six of undetermined causes.

The Temerlins, who first acquired Lucy as a two-day-old in 1965, were to become the first to raise a chimp within a completely human domestic setting, from birth to age eleven, well past sexual maturity. Previously uncharted terrain that, especially in the freewheeling, counterculture ethos of the time—one that infuses nearly every sentence of Temerlin's prose—lent the venture an air of great novelty and excitement.

By the early 1970s, Lucy was causing something of a sensation, featured in *Life, Psychology Today, Parade,* and *Science Digest* among countless other publications. She made appearances on a number of late-night TV shows, including, of course, Johnny Carson's. She'd learned to dress herself and eat with silverware at the family dinner table alongside the Temerlins' son, Steve, who was seven when Lucy was first brought into the family. She learned American Sign Language, acquiring a vocabulary of more than a hundred words. She raised her own pet cat, and mixed herself gin and tonics, which she liked to sip while sitting on the living room sofa, flipping through magazines.

The inevitable difficulties and distortions, however, of what Dr. Temerlin describes early on as "a fine undertaking" would only emerge later, thanks in no small part to *Growing Up Human,* a book that was to become an eerily appropriate companion over my coming weeks of travel among captive chimpanzees.

After thanking Lucy in his acknowledgments for her "capacity to maintain her integrity as a chimpanzee while adapting to the joys and sorrows of the human condition," Dr. Temerlin opens with an account of the accidental death of the family's previously adopted chimp, Charlie Brown. He was, it seems, playing in his enclosure in the Temerlins' backyard pet-bird sanctuary, surrounded by an audience of dozens of squawking parrots, macaws, and cockatoos, when he somehow managed to swing the makeshift blanket-hammock that he'd rigged to the upper bars of his cage into a suffocating knot.

Three weeks after Charlie Brown's death—the event Dr. Temerlin soon confesses to be an underlying motive for adopting Lucy—he and Jane decided to act on an earlier tip they'd received about a pregnant captive chimp on the East Coast. Jane flew to the pregnant chimp's side to witness the birth. The next morning, she offered the mother a Coca-Cola spiked with phencyclidine, "a drug," Dr. Temerlin writes, "that puts chimpanzees into a deep, pleasant sleep," and that very afternoon, Jane was on a return flight to Oklahoma with Lucy bundled up beside her in a bassinet, her face covered by a lacy blanket.

Tired as I was that night in Sioux City, I soon found myself eagerly turning pages. Dr. Temerlin refers in passing to Jane's "several humorous incidents on the plane as well-wishers wanted to see the baby," and then, more cryptically, to "a few tragic moments" when Jane first took the baby from her mother.

Whatever these may have been, however, Dr. Temerlin madden-ingly proclaims that "they are Jane's stories, and await her book," one that a quick check on my computer that night would reveal was either never written or never published.

All we are told is that "when mother and daughter reached home, Jane was exhausted, apprehensive, concerned about Lucy's mother's loss, and filled with doubt about her ability to meet the needs of this extremely small and independent infant." Dr. Temerlin, for his part, curiously concludes that "the airplane flight and the act of taking Lucy away from her mother had been for Jane the symbolic equivalent of the act of giving birth."

Dr. Temerlin goes on to voice a number of his own doubts and questions about the family's "adventure" with Lucy: Will she learn to love and have other human emotions as well? Would she be well-behaved, intelligent? Could he, a self-confessed momma's boy (the book is dedicated to his "Jewish mother," one chapter is titled "Chimpanzee Daughters and Jewish Mothers" and another "Oedipus-Schmedipus"), possibly make a good chim-panzee father?

The Temerlins soon find themselves dealing with all kinds of logistical nightmares as Lucy gets older, stronger, and more mischievous. She repeatedly raids the refrigerator and learns to master all the house's door locks (chimpanzees, as I also learned in my travels, are expert lock pickers), often escaping into the neighborhood or locking her parents outside for fun. She also becomes increasingly destructive and prone to temper tantrums, eventually forcing the Temerlins to build her an entire extension of the house so she can knock about her own heavily bolted quarters at will.

Still, it isn't long before the matter of Lucy's emergent sex-uality becomes the overriding concern and the primary focus of Temerlin's musings, yielding, among other things, some of the more improbable sentences I've ever come across.

"... with living organisms as highly evolved and complicated as man and chimpanzee," begins one of the passages I'd mark that first night, "the very act of observing (with whatever feeling) may change the behavior being observed. Many times this psychological Heisenberg principle has been frustrating to me, for example, when I was repeatedly unable to take pictures of Lucy masturbating with a Montgomery Ward vacuum cleaner."

A bit later in the book, while contemplating the prospect of giving up Lucy and what her future life might be without them, Dr. Temerlin writes, "I have strong feelings about the qualifications [of] the future husband of my darling virginal daughter. He would not have to be Jewish, but he would have to be gentle and patient; and he should have enough tolerance and passivity to let her take the initiative."

It was, I soon learned that night, Lucy's cruelly proscribed promiscuity that prompted Dr. Temerlin's and my own discovery of a chimp's capacity to focus on a photographic image. For the first eleven years of her life with the Temerlins, Lucy's only contact with another member of her own species was in magazine photos of herself or other chimps, although Dr. Temerlin claims she expressed no particular interest in these. He also tells of taking Lucy with the family one evening to a drive-in to see the original *Planet of the Apes.* She is said to have paid no attention to the movie whatsoever. The same, he says, held true for television.

"Lucy," Dr. Temerlin ultimately concludes, "having had all the cultural advantages since birth, has too much taste to enjoy TV, and is too happy to need escape."

And then one evening, shortly after his "daughter" had reached puberty, Temerlin notices that his son, Steve, has been collecting *Playboy* magazines, copies of which the family's housekeeper has, for whatever reason, taken to leaving on the family's living room coffee table. Dr. Temerlin, in turn, promptly takes to thumbing through the *Playboy*s with Lucy, who, he again says, showed no particular interest in them.

Dr. Temerlin, on the other hand, has very strong reactions and, of course, doesn't hesitate to share those along with his fond reminiscences of masturbating to *Playboy*s as a youth, the inspiration, he says, for his next experiment with Lucy.

Soon finding himself in an "open twenty-four hours" grocery and magazine store, he buys a copy of *Playgirl* magazine, and "with a feeling of gratitude to the Women's Liberation Movement," he returns home to find Lucy in full estrus, sitting on the sofa having a gin and tonic with Jane, "the perfect time and place," Dr. Temerlin writes, "for my experiment."

Lucy's fixation (and physical dexterity) with *Playgirl* centerfolds is soon taking up an entire chapter of *Growing Up Human*.

The last part I remember before finally falling off to sleep that night was an account of what Temerlin describes as one of Lucy's regular morning rituals on the family's living room sofa.

A remarkable, four-fisted feat of onanistic acrobatics, it involved a cup of coffee, a pocket mirror, a copy of *National Geographic* (there's no indication of which photos in particular Lucy was preoccupied with in these instances), and Lucy's one free hand, a ritual that, as Dr. Temerlin concludes, might indicate a "fragmentation of the personality" in a human being, "an inability to completely 'be there' in one's own activity. But this was "definitely not the case with Lucy."

Whatever the precise nature of Roger's preoccupation with that scroll-wielding bonobo, it seems to me in no sense sexual. Still, as I've learned once again tonight, Lucy has nothing over Roger when it comes to intensity of focus, my apparent lapse of which he now seems determined to make me regret.

Four fifteen A.M. Roger still sulking. I have no choice but to wait him out. Hold my place until he deems me worthy of his company again.

As often as I've seen him do this walk-off-wounded bit, tonight's episode has a particularly grave edge to it, owing in part, no doubt, to the strangeness of the hour, when everything seems to be taking on a scintillate life of its own—from the wall-mounted surveillance cameras just above me to the ongoing dark matter setting off the surrounding stars.

Could Roger possibly have sensed that we were making some sort of definitive progress tonight? That we were on the cusp of a major breakthrough that I then preempted by briefly drifting off? Just how tenuous an alignment is this, anyway? And how much longer can it be sustained? The ultimate stalemate when I think about it: a humanzee searching for his true identity through a human being in search of his inner chimp.

I've tried any number of things to win him back: sitting patiently by; waving the cover of *The Metaphysics of Apes* back and forth across the bedroom bars, like some obnoxious zoo-goer, hoping that the bonobo might at least draw Roger's attention. For the past few minutes I've been resorting to direct, whispered appeals, fairly begging him to return, but nothing.

Not a twitch, Roger just holding there, lost in the somnolent sway of his own hulking, cornerbound frame.

He understands a good deal of what I'm saying to him. If not all of the actual words, then certainly the lean and the ply of them. He may not have gotten the extra speech neurons we did, but I know there is another, parallel river of language flowing through that mind of his. One that I've often watched Roger dip into, sitting alone in his enclosure all day, listening to all the other retirees talking back and forth, tossing in an occasional comment of his own: this chimp who can't seem to fully recall how to be one; who can't quite time yet the slow-turning jump rope of his own original being.

Four-seventeen A.M. I've decided to turn the tables on Roger a bit, have positioned my chair so my back is to him now and will be if and when he decides to return.

I've opened *The Metaphysics of Apes* again. Am staring once more at Dr. Tulp's strange, smiley-faced wood nymph. Somehow the longer I look at it the more I keep trying to put myself in the famed anatomist's place. To inhabit Dr. Tulp's mind-set as he sat there in Stadhouder Frederick Henry's menagerie those days back in 1641, not allowing his hand to depict what his own eyes were seeing.

There are, as far as I know, no other accounts of this unwitting chimp pioneer's arrival on Europe's shores. No surviving merchant ship logs, for example, of the voyage that brought him there, although from what little I've read of the rigors of ship travel at the time, even for privileged human passengers; and with what I also know of the disposition of all chimpanzees toward any body of water above their own height—chimps can't swim; are all muscle, have no body fat; sink like stones— it's safe to say that it was one deeply disoriented and seasick fellow primate that suddenly found itself dockside at The Hague one day in 1641, bleerily inhaling the tobacco, spice, and beer-laced brine of Holland's busiest port.

The very existence of a hairy near-human such as Roger, meanwhile, would likely have induced an equivalent disorientation and queasiness in the citizenry of mid-seventeenth-century Europe, a time when a newly circumnavigated Earth was just then being dislodged by astronomers from its fixed place at the center of the universe, and the Holy Spirit evicted as well by anatomists such as Dr. Tulp from its long-established home in the chambers of the human heart.

There is no mention in *The Metaphysics of Apes* of whether any of The Hague's citizens happened to set eyes on the Stadhouder's new property before it was whisked away to his private menagerie. Still, some clues as to how people might have responded to such a sight can be found, oddly enough, in the numerous extant engravings of a far more frequent but no less startling mammalian visitation at that time along Holland's shores: beached sperm whales.

To this day, whales migrating north toward the Arctic Ocean regularly strand themselves along this same stretch of the Netherlands' eastern coast, on the North Sea. Not, it seems, due to new sonar devices but, as a number of scientists now believe, because of the disorienting effects of the frequent muddy shallows that mark that particular coastal region.

In the late sixteenth and early seventeenth centuries, however, the sudden appearance of a flailing, fifty-plus-foot-long sea creature on a local village beach was a major historical episode—in the same league as earthquakes, eclipses, comet sightings, and bouts of the plague—and, like those, still regarded more with a mind toward the event's greater symbolic significance than its specific scientific causes.

A series of whale engravings from that era appears in *An*

Embarrassment of Riches, the historian Simon Schama's study of Holland's emergence as a global power in the sixteenth and seventeenth centuries. At the very heart of each engraving there was an often strikingly realistic re-creation of the whale itself, and of the various attempts by the citizenry to, in a sense, contain and normalize the beast's very otherness: set-piece assemblages of local gentry gathered around, gesticulating; a few dwarfed figures standing either alongside or walking atop the whale, measuring everything from the length and width of the body and fins to that of the exposed penis.

But framing this central action would be all manner of exuberantly confused and invariably more mannered marginalia: from ropey, curlicue sea waves and cartoonish water-spouting whales out of medieval maps with their warnings of "Terra Incognita" and "Dragons Dwell Here" to overarching entablatures with cosmic omens and bulbous cherubs bearing scrolls of classical and biblical manuscripts.

It is easy to forget when looking at these images now that in

the absence of today's rapid-fire, multidimensional means of reporting and recording events, such elaborately staged depictions were, by and large, the entire record: beguiling combinations of factual news report and the more considered, contextualized reflections on and reconfigurations of events that one would expect to find in a novel.

But I felt from those whale engravings the same sort of tension I do when looking now at Dr. Tulp's chimp; a conflict, in a sense, between two modes of human storytelling: the symbolic and the scientific. Between two ways of thinking about and representing ourselves in the world: either as mythic subjects in some grander, predetermined allegory, or the Enlightenment's then nascent awareness of ourselves as that story's very writers and characters, decidedly unmythic and makeshift in stature.

In the brief essay that Dr. Tulp wrote about the observations he made in the Stadhouder's menagerie all those years ago, he describes his subject as "a juvenile female ape"—something one would be unlikely to ascertain either from his engraving or the title he gave to his essay: "Homo Sylvestris [Human from the Woods] Orang-outang [a local Malay word meaning roughly the same]."

"Tulp," writes Raymond Corbey in *The Metaphysics of Apes,* "was convinced that such newly discovered beings, brought back from the tropics on merchant ships, corresponded to the satyr of ancient Greek and Roman folk beliefs. [He] . . . confirmed what others before him had already suggested: the hairy, impudent Dionysian satyrs, described by ancient authors such as Pliny the Elder and familiar from literature and art, really existed. He therefore proposed calling the animal from the Stadhouder's menagerie *Satyrus indicus,* literally, satyr from the Indies."

It all sounds somewhat laughable now. And yet in many ways we haven't come all that far from Dr. Tulp's mind-set. If back in his day humanlike apes needed to be represented as satyrs, it was for not altogether unrecognizable or even unscientific reasons: to render them living cautionary tales against our own all-too-real and deeply feared animality.

Chimps, gorillas, and orangutans, as well as the Mediterranean Barbary apes, baboons, and mandrills that were known to the Greeks and Romans, had all long been portrayed in the mythologies of a number of the world's disparate, far-flung cultures as wild, lustful, primeval man-beasts, chasers and rapists of women; the very embodiments of our baser, untamed selves.

Now, some three and a half centuries later, our fellow apes are either being chained to beds to be literally raped by us, or made to misbehave at restaurant tables, and pedal around circus rings on multiseated bikes, and pull down their pants and sit on office copy machines, and sip cocktails and masturbate to magazines.

And all for the same essential reason that Dr. Tulp couldn't allow his hand to draw the actual creature seated before him in the Stadhouder's menagerie all those years ago: an ongoing inability to see animals outside of our own fraught frame of reference. To see them for who and what they really are and just let them be. The very creature that Dr. Tulp, in apprehension of modern science, tried to preserve as a mythic, half-human beast, the Temerlins, in the name of modern science, tried to make an actual human. Lost in the shuffle of either era's urgency was the animal itself.

Four twenty-two A.M. Roger is back. Sort of.

I noticed just a moment ago a shadow flit across page thirty-eight, turned, and saw Roger walking upright toward me. Then he stopped and squatted down amid the sprawl of torn Yellow Pages and old science magazines in the middle of his bedroom.

He's still there, staring blankly in my direction, his legs and feet splayed, his hands resting, palms up, on either side of him.

I've never seen this, have no idea what it might mean.

I know all the stats on the likes of Roger, their five-year-old-child's intelligence; their ability to learn and use sign language and do math fractions. How chimps recognize themselves in mirrors, as we now know dolphins and elephants do. How chimps—like us and elephants and dolphins and who knows how many other species—feel remorse and sorrow, mourning the deaths of relatives and friends.

How chimps acquire their own medicines, searching out trees the bark and leaves of which contain chemical compounds that have been found to be effective in treating the same parasites that afflict us, such as pinworm, hookworm, and giardia. And how chimps have learned to fashion and use specific tools and to pass on this knowledge to the next generation, the very essence of what we mean by the word *culture*.

Just two years ago, in fact, a pod of chimps in the jungles of southern Senegal was found to be living in caves. They retreat to them in the heat of the dry season, have picnics and siestas there, the first time in history chimps have been found to dwell in anything other than trees. The same group was later discovered to have perfected the fashioning of hunting spears, ancient artifacts of which were discovered in the ruins of settlements so recognizable they were originally mistaken for early human campsites.

I don't have children, but I've known many a five-year-old. I have very distinct memories of myself at age five. Far earlier than that, in fact, my very first memory dating back to when I was just over two years old and still in diapers, a fact for which I was mercilessly ridiculed by an aunt one day as my mother was leading me from the living room of our family's small brick row house out in Flatlands, Brooklyn, upstairs to bed, those early spindle neurons of embarrassment no doubt furiously weaving themselves into place in my brain's frontal cortex as I went.

I know all these things about our nearest kin, and yet none of it gets me any closer to Roger and what might be going through his mind; a rich fabric that I have no way of penetrating but through a kind of assertive waiting. In the same way that when I talk to Roger, I feel that I'm simply dropping stones into that parallel running river of his own thoughts and language in the hopes of setting off reverberations that he and I might both recognize.

At times I find myself thinking that if I just keep talking to him, the very flow of my words will shape, like embedded stream stones, his own brain's speech neurons. Or, better still, that if I continue writing before him tonight, I'll soon get past whatever I think I mean to remember or say. Will effectively purge my mind of the various events and emotions that have led me here to Roger by way of better discerning the ones he and I supposedly share.

I left Sioux City early in the morning, eager to cover the last forty miles or so to Royal, Nebraska. Along the town's eastern outskirts, set high above Highway 20, I came upon a giant yellow and black tiger claw scraping at the wide open air of the Great Plains, the words "Escape the World and Experience the *Wild*" scrawled below.

I pulled up directly beneath the claw, the only car in the dirt lot beside Zoo Nebraska's front gate, and stepped out into a brisk, early March wind, still feeling a bit queasy from the huge, wide-rolling dips and swells of Highway 20, my car like a tiny lifeboat on open seas.

The zoo, I soon learned from a smaller tiger-claw sign by the chain-link front gate, was closed for the season, would not reopen for another month. Somehow the idea of a "seasonal zoo" had entirely escaped my big-city-zoogoer mind-set, and now I was feeling quite ridiculous, standing out there alone on a deserted stretch of midcountry highway surrounded by miles of stubbled cornfields, a couple of scraggily wolves peering out at me from their pen on the far side of the fence as I paced back and forth beneath the giant tiger claw, trying to decide on my next course of action.

The lost chance of an impromptu visit had me in something of a bind. My hope had been to just show up as a curious traveler and make my own way to the Carson Center for Chimps to see Ripley. To have done otherwise, I'd decided—to have tried, for example, to arrange in advance for a special tour of the facility and the Carson Center—likely would have aroused suspicions about me being some sort of rabid animal rights person there to expose the zoo's fairly bleak conditions and the plight of chimps such as Ripley everywhere (all more or less true except, perhaps, for the rabid part).

Looking in from the zoo parking lot that morning, I could see no sign of Ripley or the Carson Center. Just ten feet inside the front gate was what appeared to be the visitors' center, the one that the escaped chimps had tried to enter that day: a small white clapboard house with a ticket-taker's doorsill at the front. Off to my left, in a grassless pen with a rusted water trough and some hay bales set alongside one fence, stood a lone dromedary. To my right, just behind the wolves' enclosure, a large standing birdcage contained the unmistakable loom of a vulture.

I decided to make my way around to that side of the zoo, along a narrow, house-lined dirt lane that framed the eastern terminus of Royal's tiny, four-street grid. Once beyond the wolves and the vulture, I passed in quick succession the residents of what appeared to be the rest of Zoo Nebraska's aviary collection: a winged bald eagle, a snowy owl, a red-tail hawk, and a kestrel.

At the back portion of Zoo Nebraska was a decidedly dingy, single-story, mustard-colored cement building that I figured must be the Carson Center because of its outer enclosure's jungle gyms, sandboxes, and strewn plastic toys: a caged rendition of the empty small-town park just across from where I was standing.

The Carson Center's indoor housing unit was set back a ways from the outer perimeter fence. A set of skylights atop the building and a line of narrow clerestory windows along the upper sidewalls allowed me no view inside. The sliding metal trapdoor between the indoor and outdoor enclosures was open, however, so I positioned myself as near to it as I could get and, awaiting the next lull in the wind, started to call out to Ripley, then quickly caught myself, realizing that there might be a caretaker inside the building.

My only course of action, I now decided, was to go into downtown Royal (what little there looked to be of it just up Highway 20) and ask if there might not be somebody around who would be willing to offer me—the writer of a book, I'd decided to say, about some of the country's quaintest roadside zoos—a quick guided tour.

About five hundred yards up Highway 20, past a lot filled with old abandoned Burlington-Northern Railway cars and a "Town of Royal—Population: 75" sign, stood a small service station called the Royal One-Stop, the very one, I figured, that Ripley had tried to get into that day.

I pulled up alongside its one pump. After a moment, the station-house door opened and a rugged-looking elderly gentleman wearing blue jeans and a neatly tucked plaid wool shirt came out.

"Needin' some gas?" he asked.

I told him yes, even though I'd just filled the tank before leaving Sioux City, then watched nervously as he rehitched the nozzle to the pump after only ten seconds or so.

"Didn't need much," he said.

I followed him back inside, explaining that I was being extra cautious because of the lack of gas stations in the area. I then made a point of buying a few snacks and something to drink before finally coming around to mentioning the book about roadside zoos.

"Any chance of someone showing me around Zoo Nebraska?"

"Ken should be over there right now doing some work on the place," he said, and I immediately recognized the name of the zoo director, Ken Schlueter, from the article in which I'd first read about Ripley.

"Had some bad news over there a while ago," I ventured.

"Yeah," he said. "Terrible thing."

"Were you around that day?"

He nodded. "Couple of them came down this way. I locked myself in. One chimp turned the doorknob a couple of times, then he crossed the road and climbed up that tree there."

I looked across at a huge cottonwood tree in the front yard of an old white two-story farmhouse with a wide, wraparound porch and a pair of rocking chairs on it.

"He went up to the very top, came down, and then they both started running back in the direction of the zoo."

Once back at the zoo's entrance, I noticed that there was no lock on the front gate, and it occurred to me then that there may not have been one the first time I'd approached. The place still seemed deserted—of humans at least—so I decided, with some hesitation, to let myself in.

I stopped first at the visitors' center, gave its closed front door a few knocks, thinking that Ken Schlueter might be inside. I then stepped around the side of the house and, after perusing the area yet again, started forward, my gait unsteadied now both by the fact of my trespass and the thought of the events that had transpired there.

About midway into the zoo's seven-acre grounds, a couple of scrawny mountain lions slept atop a dry-moated island. In the enclosure next to theirs was a bobcat. At what appeared to be the very heart of the facility, a pair of torpid Bengal tigers on a raised cement slab barely lifted their heads as I passed them, stopping now before a high-domed, wire-mesh enclosure. It contained a number of tall, dead, potted trees, their bundled upper branches suddenly coming alive with scurrying, bug-eyed rhesus macaques, like the startled thoughts of some huge, disembodied brain.

I was by then no more than a hundred feet from the Carson Center, and had just begun to marshal my forces for the final approach when a loud snarl sounded, then another. I turned to see the distant outline of a man seated on a bulldozer, its front shovel filled with what looked to be piles of broken limbs and branches. It seemed to be coming more or less in my direction, but I couldn't tell if the driver had spotted me, so I took a few steps into the open and raised my hand. He waved back.

Moments later, I was looking up at a big man with bulbous forearms, a scruffy beard, and wearing the same plaid-wool-shirt-and-blue-jeans combo as the service station owner. He shut off his engine. A loud gust of monkey screams rushed in to fill the sudden void.

"Just clearing some brush from the tornado."

"I didn't know there'd been one. I'm from out of town."

"Ken Schlueter," he said, hopping down and shaking my hand. "What can I do for you?"

I went directly into the roadside-zoo-book spiel, an idea that, the more I repeated it over the coming days, I found myself actually starting to like. Schlueter, for his part, listened, nodded a few times, then started walking off toward the front of the grounds, signaling me to follow with a little wave of his hand.

We started up front with the dromedary and began to work our way back, Schlueter, his burly appearance and somewhat gruff manner aside, evincing a deep, nearly childlike affection for his animals, stopping before each one, going into extended profiles that at one point spilled over into a bit of autobiography.

"I used to run an auto repair shop just over there," he said, gesturing toward the far side of Highway 20. "I started coming over here in my spare time to help out with the animals. Before I knew it I was giving up my shop and the local board of directors was appointing me to run the place."

It must have been a good half hour before Schlueter and I finally made our way to the vicinity of the Carson Center. A short ways past the macaques' enclosure, I noticed a painted wooden "Carson Center" sign, faded and broken in some brush beside the center's front entrance ramp. Schlueter was making no further movements toward the place, and I was now beginning to think there was nobody inside; that Ripley had perhaps gone mad in the wake of the recent shootings and either needed to be put down or had simply died from grief.

"And that would be the Carson Center," I finally said, the force of nearly two thousand miles of driving and months of speculation about Ripley finally surmounting both my own and Schlueter's natural circumspection.

Schlueter nodded, mumbled something inaudible, and then the two of us made our way toward the entrance. We passed through a metal door into a narrow glassed-off viewing area opposite a series of adjacent barred enclosures, all of them empty. I noticed that each of the trapdoors between them was ajar, just like the one farthest to the right in the wall leading to the outer enclosure, and I knew now that the only possibility of Ripley being on the premises was if he'd happened to slip through that last door to the outside just as Schlueter and I were coming up the entrance ramp.

Schlueter started pointing out the different design features of the Carson Center's cage construction, the feeding portholes, door latches, and sliding trapdoor mechanisms, variations of which I'd become more familiar with in the coming weeks than I'd ever hoped to. I figured this to be a kind of avoidance tactic on Schlueter's part, a way of delaying the onset of the dark memories there, so I stood patiently by, asking questions, even taking out a notepad at one point to jot down some details "for the book."

When we finally got to the door at the other end of the viewing area, Schlueter held it open for me. I took a deep breath, stepped back outside, and turned to see the same disengaged array of primate recreational fixtures I'd been looking at just before from the far side of the fence.

Schlueter paused, took out and lit a cigarette, then leaned his big forearms on the railing before him, staring off in the direction of the town park. This seemed to me as good a time as any.

"Heard only one survived," I said.

"Yeah," he replied, sighing deeply. "Not a good day."

It was, he went on to explain, a young, untrained volunteer helper who'd failed to adequately secure the Carson Center's outer enclosure that morning. The lock, it seems, had never been fully closed, and the chimps were instantly aware of it.

"They never heard that click," Schlueter said, his voice becoming animated now with the very memory of his former charges' cleverness. "And you know what? They still waited a few hours, until there was no one around, before they made their break."

I would hear of this sort of thing over and over in the coming weeks, what ingenious lock pickers and escape artists our closest ape cousins can be. In *Growing Up Human*, Dr. Temerlin tells of Lucy getting past a locked kitchen door by unbolting the hinges. She also used the key-secreted-in-the-mouth trick a number of times to get out of her specially built quarters and wreak havoc in the house after the Temerlins went out. Once, as Dr. Temerlin briefly stepped onto his back porch naked after a shower, Lucy crept up and locked the door behind him, forcing him to scramble around to an open front window to let himself back in.

Patti Ragan says she is maniacal about checking and double-checking the locks around here. I have read of one infamous orangutan-Houdini named Henry at a zoo in Minnesota who'd gotten so good at escaping his enclosure there that the zookeeper eventually incorporated his ape's talents into a wildly popular shtick in which Henry would perform one of his escapes and carry around the zookeeper in his arms for a while. Henry would then return to his pen, place the zookeeper back outside, politely close the door and relock himself inside.

Schlueter straightened up a moment and gestured for me to follow him. We walked around to the outdoor enclosure's door, a two-inch-thick, four-foot-wide metal slab. He demonstrated how, even with an inadequately secured lock, one of the chimps had to have stuck his arm through the nearest aperture in the bars and reached across the entire width of the door to get at the lock. Then, with the very tips of his fingers, he had to pull the lock open before twisting and lifting it back up through a three-tiered latch.

"Pretty impressive, huh?"

Much of what followed, Schlueter told me, was still kind of a blur in his mind. He said he heard some screams, came running out of the visitors' center, and saw, essentially, a zoo director's worst nightmare: his four chimpanzees madly running about the grounds as people, some of them with young children, were trying to find someplace to take cover.

He made an immediate call to the Antelope County Sheriff's Department, then hopped in his golf cart and started racing about the grounds, trying at once to keep the chimps away from his patrons and quickly herd the latter into the zoo's visitors' center.

"I bumped a couple of the chimps with the front of the cart," he told me. "I was just trying anything to keep them off."

We tend, as I say, to think of chimpanzees as cute, wholly benign creatures in large part because of the very role we now co-opt them to play. Their entrapment is, in this sense, more inescapable and multichambered than any of our locks. If once they were construed as animate cautionary tales, the scary embodiments of our own barely constrained bestial nature, we've since come to celebrate our perceived triumph over that beastliness by employing them for comic relief: miniversions of ourselves in civilized settings, running playfully amok.

Somewhat unbelievably, just six months prior to that September morning's outbreak at Zoo Nebraska, two former chimp entertainers named Buddy and Ollie, chimps who grew up with and were trained for show business alongside Ripley, had broken out of their retirement facility, a privately owned animal sanctuary known as Animal Haven Ranch, in the Southern California town of Caliente.

Ripley, Buddy, and Ollie all belonged to a West Coast–based animal trainer who recently decided to get out of the business (he claims to have gotten tired of the constant harassment from animal rights groups) and decided to surrender all of his still-active chimps here to the Center for the Great Apes rather than selling them for profit to other trainers.

Sixteen-year-old Buddy and thirteen-year-old Ollie were living with two other chimps at Animal Haven Ranch the day they broke free. In the enclosure next door to theirs was Moe, a former pet chimpanzee whose "parents," St. James and La Donna Davis, had just arrived at Animal Haven Ranch to celebrate, as they did every year, the now thirty-nine-year-old Moe's birthday.

The Davises were apparently standing in front of Moe's enclosure, the sixty-two-year-old St. James Davis holding a birthday cake, when something—the cake, the lit candles atop it, a gesture made by St. James Davis, his appearance, his tone of voice—set Buddy off.

It isn't clear how Buddy got out, but it seems that just as happened at the Carson Center, someone had not adequately secured a lock. La Donna Davis tried to protect her husband. Buddy bit her thumb, then set upon St. James, biting off his nose and lips, an eye, part of his cheek, both testicles, and one of his feet. According to a medic at the scene, Davis's face was entirely gone.

The son-in-law of Animal Haven's owner grabbed the shotgun that was kept on the premises and shot Buddy dead. When Buddy's mate, the thirteen-year-old Ollie, then ran out of their enclosure, took hold of the severely injured Davis, and started off down the road with him toward a nearby patch of woods, Ollie was shot dead as well.

Ken Schlueter told me that he had only a tranquilizer gun on the premises the morning when Ripley and the others broke free. He said that he kept it precisely for such emergencies, but that owing to the size of the two chimps he tried to bring down—Reuben and Jimmy Joe, each weighing more than two hundred pounds—and the amount of adrenaline they probably had running through them at the time, the drugs seemed to have little effect.

"They were pretty worked up," Schlueter recalled. "After five minutes, there was still no sign of them slowing down. They were running around like crazy. One nearly got to a mother and her child as they were heading for cover, but I managed to bump him just in time with my cart. Another one of them ran over to the visitors' center and started ripping the air conditioner out of the window. He nearly had the thing off, and the people inside were screaming. That's when I grabbed the sheriff's revolver."

I could see Schlueter struggling a bit with his emotions, but the memory had full hold of him by then and demanded completion. Tyler, he told me, the chimp who'd gone into town with Ripley, was the first one he shot. He said it then started to look like Jimmy Joe, whom Schlueter described as the self-appointed patriarch and protector of the group, was trying to round the others up to get them back to the Carson Center. At least, Schlueter told me, that's the way he remembers it now, with the painful clarity that distance affords.

"Jimmy Joe seemed to be trying to get them together," he repeated. "But Tyler made a sudden wrong turn, went the opposite way, and I brought him down near the visitors' center."

Reuben he remembered shooting as he and Ripley were heading back in the general direction of the Carson Center, with Jimmy Joe flanking them on the left.

"I shot Jimmy Joe there," he said, pointing to the ground right alongside where he and I were standing. "He kept . . ."

Schlueter lit another cigarette and then looked away.

"He kept trying to raise himself up," he said, his voice choking. "I really think now he was still trying to protect the others."

It was just then, Schlueter said, that Ripley came running up from behind him, actually vaulted off Schlueter's back, bounded across the top of the Carson Center's outside enclosure, and then let himself back inside through the still open metal door.

"Just like that," Schlueter said, snapping his fingers. "Never seen anything like it in my life."

I felt certain now that I was about to get the final word on Ripley, that he had, in fact, succumbed to the trauma of seeing his companions gunned down, the stories rushing through my head now of other chimps who'd lost their minds and/or their will to live in the wake of traumatic occurrences: longtime lab subjects suffering from nervous breakdowns; ongoing episodes of self-imposed starvation and self-mutilation, plucking all their own body hair out; and bouts of what's known as "dissociative floating hand and foot syndrome," during which they'll focus for so long on either their hand or foot that they start to behave as though the limb doesn't belong to them any longer, screaming in fear at it, attacking and biting it, sometimes gnawing it off altogether.

There is, too, the story that Dr. Christiaan Barnard, the late pioneering heart transplant surgeon, relates in his book *Good Life, Good Death* of an incident in the course of a trial transplant procedure he'd performed back in the 1960s with a chimpanzee heart. He and some assistants went to the holding facility in which two lab chimps were being kept in adjacent cells. They proceeded to sedate one chimp and remove him for the operation in full view of his cellmate. That chimp went fully berserk, screaming and crying, knocking his head against the bars.

"The other chimpanzee wept bitterly," Barnard wrote, "and was inconsolable for days. I vowed never again to experiment with such sensitive creatures."

I stood there beside Ken Schlueter, watching him finish his cigarette. Then he straightened up a moment and turned toward me.

"I probably should be getting back to work," he said, reaching to shake my hand, then starting off toward his tractor.

"And Ripley?" I called out.

"Oh," Schlueter said, "we sent him to another facility."

They almost invariably end this way, zoo breakouts: with the stark finality of frontier justice.

Even when the frontier and the justice are entirely man-made and the final verdict fixed.

Even when we are the ones who cross over the painted red line, who break into their space.

I remember one hot spring night in my Brooklyn neighborhood twenty years ago when a couple of kids decided to go for a swim in the polar bears' moat over at Prospect Park Zoo, just up the block from my apartment building. I'd heard the distant sounds of gunfire and police sirens that evening, but that having been a more or less regular occurrence in my neighborhood at that time, I didn't find out about the incident until I picked up the newspapers at the corner store the following day.

The police, responding to calls about screams from inside the zoo, arrived to find the bears pawing at the lifeless body of one of the boys. Thinking that he might still be alive, or that the other boy could be hiding somewhere inside the lair, the officers went to their patrol car for shotguns, came back, and blew the bears away.

I've thought about that night often, about what made those

boys choose the polar bears' moat. They could have far more easily and safely cooled off in the zoo's nearby, wide-open seal pool. They, however, chose to clamber up the high, spiked bars of the polar bears' enclosure to get to what they believed to be the coldest water. Or the moat of the animal that most readily symbolizes "coldness," the one pictured on the ice cube bags and soft drink bottles. The actual bears were lost, in the boys' minds, to what they have come to represent.

Children, we say to ourselves now, are far more apt to view animals in such a symbolic way, to regard them within an entirely human frame of reference. And yet for much of history, that is precisely how animals have been viewed by us: either as emissaries of that purer primeval world from which our own added spindle cells have seemingly exiled us, or as embodiments of the very beastliness that those same added brain cells have supposedly enabled us to rise above.

I read not long ago about a bizarre fresco that once covered an entire wall of the Church of the Holy Trinity in the ancient French city of Falaise in Normandy. Originally composed in the fourteenth century on the west wall of the church's south transept, the painting was whitewashed over in the early 1820s—owing, it is said, to a long-standing embarrassment and discomfort over its content. A short time later the wall itself was largely destroyed by renovations.

The fresco depicted a major event in Falaise's public square in January 1386: the execution of a sow for the crime of infanticide. The animal had been given a full trial in the local town court, found guilty, and sentenced to death by hanging, though not before a prescribed public mangling and maiming of the offender's head and forelegs, this in retribution for the severe disfigurements the sow had caused to the face and arms of the child it had killed.

The only surviving visual account of the event—a nineteenth-century lithograph based on numerous written descriptions compiled over the years of the original Falaise fresco—serves as the frontispiece for a long-out-of-print historical text I came upon while researching the story about the current collapse of elephant culture, a book titled *The Criminal Prosecution and Capital Punishment of Animals: The Lost History of Europe's Animal Trials.*

Written by the British historian E. P. Evans and first published in 1906, the book traces the long history (dating back at least to the ancient Greeks) of putting animals on trial for their perceived crimes: elaborate, drawn-out courtroom dramas in which the accused—everything from infanticidal sows to thieving caterpillars, grain-filching rats, and chirping sparrows accused of disrupting church services—would be accorded the same legal rights as human beings, right down to being provided with the best available defense attorneys, and all at the taxpayers' expense.

In the re-creation of the execution in Falaise in 1386, the sow is shown atop the gallows in the town's crowded public square, seated upright on a wooden stool, dressed in a man's jacket and breeches. A robed magistrate stands directly alongside the animal, reading out the tribunal of Falaise's sentence, the first part of which the town's hooded hangman seems to be in the process of carrying out. He's kneeling behind the strapped-down guilty party with a pair of pincers in one hand, a taut neck chain in the other, the sow's head thrown far back, its mouth opened in apparent agony.

There is a translated copy of the hangman's receipt in an appendix at the back of the book, dated January 9, 1386, in which the hangman acknowledges having been paid by the viscount of Falaise "ten sous and ten deniers tournois for the execution of an infanticidal sow. . . ." He is also given an additional "ten sous tournois" with which to buy a pair of new gloves, so

that he might "come away from the discharge of his duty . . . with clean hands, thus indicating that as a minister of justice, he incurred no guilt in shedding blood."

In his book, Evans also compiled from available historical records a partial, twenty-page chronology of Europe's animal trials and executions over the centuries. It begins with the sentencing and summary execution of some moles in the Valley of Aosta in the year 824 and ends with the 1906 trial, covered in the *Echo de Paris* and in the *New York Herald,* of a dog in Switzerland.

The dog was accused of being an accomplice to the robbery and murder of a man named Marger by a father-son criminal tandem known as the Scherrers. All three were tried for murder. The Scherrers were sentenced to life imprisonment. Their dog, however, "without whose complicity the crime could not have been committed," was condemned to death.

In the eleven centuries between the condemning of the Aosta moles and the Scherrers' dog, every imaginable earthly creature was tried and sentenced in a human court of law, from she-asses, eels, horses, and dolphins to all manner of villainous vermin: rats, weevils, locusts, worms, snails, horseflies, and Spanish flies.

When, as was often the case with rodents and insects, the guilty parties were too widely dispersed to appear in court, they were tried in absentia. And when a person was accused of copulating with an animal, both parties would be tried, sentenced, and executed together, a practice that was carried over from the Old World to the New.

The American clergyman Cotton Mather records in his writings that "on June 6th, 1662, at New Haven, there was a most unparalleled wretch, one Potter by name, about sixty years of age, executed for damnable bestialities." Described as a long-time, pious member of the church "devout in worship, gifted in prayer, forward in edifying discourse among the religious, and zealous in reforming the sins of other people," he was nevertheless discovered to have "lived in most infandous Buggeries for no less than fifty years . . . and now at the gallows there were killed before his eyes a cow, two heifers, three sheep and two sows, with all of which he had committed his brutalities."

Many young lawyers, meanwhile, made their names from the inspired defenses they mounted for their creaturely clients, cases in which they not only established legal precedents for future human court proceedings, but often either got their animal defendants off on lesser charges or freed outright.

Evans writes of one distinguished sixteenth-century French jurist named Bartholomew Chassenee, who helped forge his reputation as a brilliant defense strategist after being appointed in his very first case to be legal counsel for a bevy of rats that had been brought to trial in the ecclesiastical court of Autun for having destroyed the province's barley crop.

Among the tactics employed by Chassenee was to argue that

because the defendants were dispersed over such a broad swath of country and dwelled in so many different villages, a single summons was insufficient to notify them all. Then, in the course of the considerable time it would take for the courts to obtain a second summons, one that was to be pronounced from the pulpits of all the parishes in which the accused rats resided, Chassenee mounted a successful defense of his clients' inevitable failure to appear in court, expounding at great length about both the distance and the perils of their journey, owing in no small part "to the unwearied vigilance of their mortal enemies, the cats."

It all tends to read today like absurdist allegory, the manifestation, we tell ourselves, of a more mythic, childlike mind-set. Of a kind of deep naïveté that has long since been outgrown by us and more or less whitewashed, like that fresco in Falaise, from our collective memory. Evans, for his part, sees these proceedings more as "show trials," purposefully symbolic rituals, ways of purging evil sprits and imposing order on a seemingly chaotic world, a theory somewhat belied by the elaborately earnest and precise legalese of the cases and the many precedents they produced.

But whatever the various impulses behind such trials might have been, they are neither so unrecognizable nor so remote as we might think. Just before setting off for Uganda to research the increasingly aberrant behaviors of wild elephants, I was reading about similar behaviors that have long been observed among their captive counterparts (the fact that the pathologies of wild and captive elephants have come to exactly mirror each other says, well, everything) and came at one point upon the story of a five-ton Asian elephant named Mary.

Part of a small traveling circus in the United States, Mary was impounded in September 1916 by a local sheriff in Tennessee for killing a young hotel janitor who'd been hired to mind

Mary during a stopover in the northeastern Tennessee town of Kingsport. Apparently the janitor had taken Mary for a swim at a local pond, where, according to witnesses, he poked her behind the ear with a metal hook just as she was reaching for a piece of floating watermelon rind. Enraged, Mary turned, swiftly snatched her minder up with her trunk, dashed him against a refreshment stand, and then smashed his head with her foot.

With cries from the townspeople to "Kill the elephant!" and threats from nearby town leaders to bar the circus if "Murderous Mary," as newspapers quickly dubbed her, remained a part of the show, the circus's owner, Charlie Sparks, knew he had to do something to appease the public's bloodlust and save his business.

Among the sentences he is said to have contemplated was electrocution, a ghastly precedent for which had been set thirteen years earlier, on the grounds of the nearly completed Luna Park in Coney Island, Brooklyn. A longtime circus elephant there named Topsy, who'd killed three trainers in as many years—the last one after he tried to feed her a lighted cigarette—became the largest and most prominent victim of Thomas Edison, the father of direct-current electricity, who had already publicly executed a number of animals at that time using his rival George Westinghouse's alternating current, in hopes of discrediting it as being too dangerous.

Sparks ultimately decided to have Mary hanged, shipping her by train to the nearby town of Erwin, Tennessee, where more than twenty-five hundred people gathered at the local rail yard for her execution. Dozens of children are said to have run off screaming in terror when the hanging chain that was suspended from a huge industrial crane snapped, leaving Mary writhing on the ground with a broken hip. A local rail worker promptly clambered up Mary's bulk and secured a heavier chain for a second, successful hoisting.

This took place less than a hundred years ago. Somehow, Mary's and Topsy's stories—like those of the sow in the Falaise fresco and of Bartholomew Chassenee's acquitted rats; or of those mannerly engraved whales, and Dr. Tulp's chimp satyr; and the likes of Lucy and Ripley and Roger—are all aspects of the same ongoing struggle on our part to configure our own rightful place among animals. All manifestations of a mind still stranded, like those beached whales, somewhere between the mythic and the matter-of-fact.

The great irony is that were the likes of Mary, or Buddy and Ollie, or Zoo Nebraska's Ripley to be accorded today the same legal privileges as their medieval counterparts, the most amateur lawyer would be able to get them all off on insanity pleas.

A modern-day Bartholomew Chassenee, meanwhile, would have entire courtrooms weeping, the signature difference about this particular moment in the history of our relationship with the animals being that where once we had to impose our stories upon them to better understand ourselves, now we have only to tell the animals' stories.

Four thirty A.M. Something is up with Roger. Something I don't remember hearing described as one of his neurotic ticks, and that he has certainly never done with me before.

He has begun to lift cupped handfuls of air from the right side of him and then put them down on his left, one by one, in very caring and deliberate measures, like a child in a sandbox. Every so often one or two handfuls will go up over his left shoulder, as though they contain something offensive in his mind or at least are not worthy of conserving, and then he resumes the careful side-piling again.

Whatever this may be about, I've no intention of interrupting it. He seems to be in such a deep trance, reliving and reveling in one of his fondest memories, for all I know, playing in the yard, perhaps, as a baby chimp with his life's one chimpanzee friend, Sally.

Maddening, at times, the proximity of so much unspoken meaning and motive. But I have learned to just take it. To remain in uncertainty and incomprehension without impatiently reaching for and imposing on Roger any motives or meanings of my own.

He is, after all, my escort past the usual entrapments of our brain's added spindle cells: things such as linear logic, reason, direct causality. And once beyond those, one is literally in no-man's-land. Once there—and Roger, even now, even in his own entranced state, can tell whether you are truly at home within the spell of an abided blankness—you can only keep going forward feelingly, can only proceed by what I've come to think of between myself and Roger as a kind of osmotic inference.

Upon leaving Ken Schlueter and Zoo Nebraska that after-noon, I remember feeling as I imagine Ripley must have the day he and the others broke free, perched high atop that cottonwood tree in downtown Royal, taking one long look at the surround-ing blankness and then scampering back to the only refuge he knew. I had, in effect, gone thousands of miles out of my way to arrive at the physical epicenter of a metaphysical malaise, the latter somehow only beginning to come into focus upon achieving the former.

I promptly recrossed the wide-rolling swells of Highway 20, and checked back into the same Sioux City motel at about dusk. Up in my room, I poured myself some whiskey and started to think hard about what I was doing and what I might want to do next. But it wasn't long before the realization that I had little idea of either began to fill me with a nearly transcen-dent thrill. The very pointlessness of my predicament had now become the point, an achievement in and of itself, the comple-tion of the early stage of some larger plan I wouldn't even begin to recognize until that moment last week when Roger clapped his hands and reminded me, in a sense, of just how tired I had, in fact, become of being only a man.

I phoned Bex back in Brooklyn to tell her that Ripley was no longer at Zoo Nebraska.

She told me to come home.

I said I wasn't sure, that I had to think about it, that I'd come an awfully long way to just turn around and start back now. Then I hung up and remembered how hungry I was.

Not wanting to venture far for dinner, I ended up walking over to the same barbecue joint where I'd eaten the night before. I took a seat at the bar, ordered a drink and some dinner, pulled out my copy of *Growing Up Human,* and opened furtively to the page I'd left off at the night before: Dr. Temerlin, in a chapter titled "On Incest and Oedipus" explaining that while he never experienced sexual desire for Lucy (although he does admit to frequently letting Lucy mouth his penis), he did have fantasies of Lucy making sexual advances toward him, and of his artificially impregnating her with his semen.

Such "fantasies" are hardly original to Dr. Temerlin. Recent comparisons of the newly completed chimp and human genomes done by a team of scientists at Harvard indicate that there must have been cross-species commingling between the earliest ancestors of the modern chimp and human lineages, probably saving the human race from early extinction due to sterility in the first protohuman males.

We humans, in other words, are not merely 99 percent the same as chimps. We may well owe our very existence to primeval intercourse with them, something we've been reenacting, in both mythology and reality, ever since. Dr. Tulp's Dionysian chimp-human satyr is, it seems, not so much a willful conceit as a deep cellular memory.

Sex with apes, while not generally a matter of public record, has gone on for ages, from the palm oil workers raping orangutans to long-ago and elaborately staged acts of public bestiality featured in Roman games and circuses, "events" involving a range of creatures from leopards and wild boars to jackasses, dogs, and finally apes. Typically mandrills or baboons, they would be made drunk with wine and then loosed upon groups of young girls, most often virgins, whose genitals had been soaked with the female urine of either a mandrill or a baboon.

As for the possibility of a human impregnating a chimpanzee (or vice versa) and producing a viable offspring, the chances are greatly complicated by the discrepancy in the number of chromosomes between the two species, chimps possessing twenty-four pairs and humans twenty-three. Still, a chimp-human hybrid, though likely to be sterile, is biologically feasible, and there has been all manner of speculation and lurid lore over the ages about the existence of actual "humanzees" or "chumans" or "manpanzees."

Back in the eleventh century, St. Peter Damian wrote of one Count Guliemus, whose pet ape became his wife's lover. The ape apparently became "mad with jealousy" upon seeing the count one day in bed with his wife—much as Dr. Temerlin describes Lucy behaving whenever she saw him and Jane lying together—and fatally attacked the count. Damian goes on to claim that he was told of this by none other than Pope Alexander II, who also is said to have then shown Damian a creature named Maimo, the putative hybrid offspring of the ape and the countess's coupling.

More recent humanzee lore contains stories of a female chimpanzee that was impregnated with human sperm in a laboratory in a remote Chinese village in the 1940s, but that chimp, in what sounds like a neat recapitulation of Mary Shelley's *Frankenstein,* was reportedly killed and the laboratory burned down by a mob of angry villagers. Similarly, a doctor in Shenyang, in northeastern China, is claimed to have successfully inseminated a female chimpanzee with human sperm, but the three-month-old fetus was destroyed along with the doctor's lab by Red Guards. Another human-chimp hybrid was supposedly created in the 1930s at the former Yerkes National Primate

Research Center in Orange Park, Florida, and then subsequently destroyed by scientists there.

But perhaps the world's best-known "humanzee" was making headlines at exactly the same time as Dr. Temerlin's Lucy. Oliver, often referred to in his heyday as "the missing link," started out, like Roger, as a circus performer who from a very early age preferred the company of humans to that of his fellow chimps. Oliver's appearance alone—tall and thin with an unusually small, bald head; pointy, batlike ears; and a fully upright, bipedal walk—made him seem decidedly other.

But it was Oliver's overall demeanor and mannerisms that most captivated people: the way he'd sit upright and cross-legged in chairs, wielding his morning cup of coffee or personally mixed tumbler of bourbon and 7UP; or how he'd go about his circus trainer's property with a wheelbarrow, emptying hay and straw from the stalls; or watch TV and, at certain dramatic scenes, occasionally break with his strangely birdlike voice into high-pitched sobs.

Oliver's emergent sexuality, the story goes, soon had him making repeated advances on his trainer's wife, and he was thus promptly sold to the first of a series of owners eager to capitalize on Oliver's uniqueness. By the mid-1970s, the cigar-smoking, sherry-swilling "missing link" was flying on chartered 747s and making TV appearances around the world. He did *The Ed Sullivan Show,* among others, and was a long-running smash hit on Japan's Nippon TV.

Oliver would eventually end up in the hands of a number of different West Coast animal trainers, owners of roadside attractions with names such as Enchanted Village or Gentle Jungle, where he was featured as the "half-man, half-ape" star of freak shows. But after the last of his owners closed down his place in 1986, Oliver was dispatched to a research lab facility in

Pennsylvania for seven years before finally landing in a small, private primate sanctuary outside San Antonio, Texas, where he resides to this day. It wasn't until 1995 that scientists from the University of Chicago finally conducted a test of Oliver's DNA and concluded that, his peculiar traits and mannerisms aside, Oliver is all chimpanzee.

Still, while evidence of actual humanzees has been scant, there is no longer much doubt about real attempts to create one, and in some cases in rather spectacular fashion. Secret documents recently uncovered in state archives after the fall of the Soviet Union have revealed that in the mid-1920s Joseph Stalin enlisted Russia's top animal-breeding scientist, Ilya Ivanov, the father of artificial insemination, to conduct a series of "interspecies hybridization experiments" with the intention of creating what Stalin envisioned as an invincible *Planet of the Apes*–like army of humanzees with superhuman strength and stamina.

Put in the form of an official request from the Politburo to the Academy of Science in 1926, the plan was to create both a "living war machine" to bolster the then beleaguered Red Army, and a new labor force for the Soviet Union's first Five-Year Plan to build a modern industrialized and egalitarian society.

"I want a new invincible human being," Stalin is quoted in Russian newspapers as having instructed Ivanov, "insensitive to pain, resistant and indifferent about the quality of food they eat."

Ivanov arranged an expedition to the western African nation of Guinea in March 1926 to conduct his experiments. Despite repeated failures at impregnating chimpanzees with human sperm, Ivanov was reportedly convinced that he'd have no trouble enlisting local women to be inseminated with chimp sperm, but could find no one willing to participate.

Upon his return to the Soviet Union, Ivanov continued his hybridization experiments at a newly established primate station in Sukhumi, Georgia. He had intended to impregnate five human volunteers there, but the only mature male chimp at Sukhumi died before the plan could be carried out. In the course of waiting for new chimp recruits, Ivanov and a number of fellow scientists involved in the experiments fell victim to a political shakeup in Moscow. Ivanov eventually lost his position and in 1930 was sentenced to five years of exile in Kazakhstan, where he died of a stroke in 1932.

Dreams of compliant, indefatigable humanzee laborers, however, did not die with Ivanov. In a 1974 book by Belgian zoologist Bernard Heuvelmans and Soviet scientist Boris F. Porshnev titled *The Neanderthal Man Is Alive and Well,* there is an account of a Russian doctor who escaped from a Soviet concentration camp and sometime in the early 1950s met with a friend of Heuvelmans. The doctor said he'd been arrested for refusing to obey orders from his superiors to impregnate Oriental women in forced labor camps with the sperm of male gorillas. The experiment, according to the doctor, went forward regardless, and a number of successful hybrids were created. Far larger than the average human and covered in fur, they were described as being tireless salt-mine workers who, due to genetic mutations, were nevertheless at once sterile and short-lived.

"Good book?"

I looked up from my Sioux City barstool at a man who appeared to be in his early forties, dressed in a snap-buttoned denim shirt, blue jeans, and cowboy boots, a carefully etched goatee framing his pursed lips and square jaw. Thankfully, my copy of *Growing Up Human* had no jacket, had been shipped to me without one, so all that my curious companion could see was the book's blank, bright red cover.

"Yes," I said.

I've often found in instances like these that where just a bit of diffidence on my part would likely disabuse anyone of the assumption that I want to converse, some admixture of my own vanity and reportorial curiosity always compels me to further engage the very person I'd rather flee.

I spared this guy, of course, the details of Dr. Temerlin's doings in *Growing Up Human*. But I did use the book's general subject matter to go on at some length about my own pursuits, my attempt to find Ripley, and about the number of captive chimpanzees in the United States, all the while replaying in my mind an eerily similar encounter I'd recently had near the very end of my travels in Uganda to write about elephants.

I had just returned to my lodge in western Uganda's Queen Elizabeth National Park after a day of elephant tracking. I got cleaned up in my room and was on the way to the bar to get a beer when I passed a small meeting area off the lodge veranda behind a pair of nearly drawn curtains. There were rows of folding chairs inside set before a large TV that had been rigged up to show World Cup soccer matches in which a number of African teams were still competing at the time. Not certain at first if this was somebody's private affair, I took a closer look and, seeing no one inside, I went and got my beer, came back, and slipped into the last row of seats.

I can't recall now what teams were playing, only that after ten minutes or so, a few more people wandered in, and then in one big rush, a contingent of what, judging from their appearance, accents, and conversation, I guessed to be a group of midwestern American college kids on some sort of a field biology junket. I was intent on keeping to myself, but it wasn't long before one of them was turning in my direction in that same upbeat, forthright manner as my Sioux City barmate.

"Here on safari?" he asked.

My vanity, in this instance, compelled me to distinguish

myself from the ranks of mere safari tourists, and it wasn't long before I was mentioning, in as offhanded a manner as I could muster, the story I was researching about "psychotic elephants," I think I called them, just to spice things up a bit.

In no time, the entire group was turned my way, questions flying. With the help of a few more beers, I was soon going on and on, telling the story of how we humans are systematically destroying elephant culture, inevitably leading me to talk of the similar plight of chimpanzees, and then to broader musings about, among other things, our deep biological bonds with all creatures. I even managed to segue into a recent story I'd written about the newly emergent science of "animal personality," in which researchers from a broad array of disciplines are now detecting all the different aspects of our individual personalities, things such as sociability or shyness, aggressiveness or timorousness, in creatures from primates to the merest paramecium.

At one point—I think via a discussion of the elephant brain versus our own—a number of my new companions started talking about the human body's different organs and what complex biological entities each one of those is. Nodding his head vigorously, the kid who'd first introduced himself to me then began telling the story of how he had recently donated the right lobe of his liver to his younger brother, who was dying of a rare form of liver disease, an increasingly common transplant procedure now in which, the liver being the only part of our body that can regenerate itself, both the donor and the recipient develop full livers again in as few as three to four months after the surgery.

"The surgeon who did the operation," the kid said, sitting forward in his seat, his eyes widening, "told me something amazing. He said that organs are so sensitive that if he were to even touch someone's stomach during an operation, the stomach would feel the impact of that for more than a year afterward."

A sort of reverent silence seized the room, and although I'd never heard anything quite like that before, I was soon launching into my own reverie about the vast amount of time it took for evolution to even concoct something like our stomach, and how removed we humans tend to be from such primordial particulars of our own biology.

From the fact that every part of us is, in the end, the compendium of billions of years of biological borrowings: our hearts, for example, which evolution, like some workshop-bound artificer, fashioned from countless prior cardiac templates and other long-ago patented parts, right down to using for our heart muscle's prodigious pumping power the same molecular motor that keeps a fly's wings beating more than 150 times a second.

Or the fact that the different microorganisms that look and function like miniature bodily organs within each one of our body's cells (and everyone sitting there around me that evening knew their names, the "mitochondria," the "ribosomes," and so on; the very organisms that power our cells and govern all of the functions that allow our lives to happen) are themselves each direct descendants of the very first bacterial life-forms that, for billions of years on Earth, were the only life on this planet.

"We, in other words," I declaimed at one point, "carry within each of our body's cells the definitive fossil evidence, or 'living fossils' of our and all life's descent from Earth's very first bacteria, the very evidence that some are still claiming the 'theory' of evolution lacks."

On and on I went, piling up air just like Roger here: how we self-important humans with our illusion-inducing extra neuronal threads are ultimately mere motes on the eyelash of the body of all those billions of years of biology that both preceded and prefigured us; and how if we as a species (and here I was really going for broke, as though looking to recruit my young science-minded cronies for some sort of new crusade on behalf of science's inherent mystique and spirituality) could only learn to redirect our collective heavenward gazes downward and inward, we would, paradoxically, find consoling intimations of the infinite and the eternal in the very minutiae of our own and of all life's makeup.

It was, I suppose, the sound of my own voice that at last arrested this rant. I briefly noticed my own hands still gesticulating against the silence, and then looked up to find myself more or less pinned in place by an array of shrouded, dead-eyed stares, like a bunch of just-touched turtle heads that had all withdrawn into their carapaces.

The entire group then stood and, one by one, quietly filed out of the room, a last voice calling out from between the wafting curtains something that sounded to me like "Six days, dude. . . . He did it all in six days," words I didn't fully make sense of until I'd gone around the corner for some dinner on the veranda a short while later and saw from my table the entire group, standing fully clad in the nearby lodge swimming pool, performing baptisms and singing praises to the Lord.

I had taken care in front of my Sioux City barmate that night not to tip my hand so readily, restricting myself to generic chimp and roadside zoo stories and to the book I was hoping to write.

"I heard about those Zoo Nebraska chimps," he interrupted. "I got a place along Highway 20 between here and Royal. Tell you what. If any of those chimps had made it as far as my land I'd have shot them straightaway, no hesitation. Wild animals. Powerful. People forget that."

I nodded.

"Know what's funny," he went on. "That people believe we could have descended from them."

"Yeah," I muttered, somewhat incredulous now that I'd stepped into the same lair twice in such a short period of time.

I was soon getting the usual spiel about all the flaws in the theory of evolution, the arrogance of its proponents, the "gaps" in the fossil evidence, and so on.

And then things got really scary: detailed reenactments of scenes from a documentary he'd seen, scenes so ludicrous-sounding that upon returning to my motel room that evening—I would quickly finish my drink at the bar and repair to a table to have dinner in peace—I went to my computer, typed in something along the lines of "evangelicals on apes," and there it was, Kirk Cameron and Ray Comfort's "The Way of the Master" website.

The Evolution Zone, one among a number of "The Way of the Master" films listed, opens with a wide-eyed, baby-faced Cameron doing a particularly lousy imitation of Rod Serling from *The Twilight Zone,* introducing us in this instance to bizarre delusions and distortions of Darwin's theory, followed soon thereafter by the scenes of Cameron and Comfort sitting at a restaurant table on either side of the salad-strewing, tablecloth-chomping Bam Bam.

As often as I've asked myself who or what exactly we have made of creatures such as Roger, I've also wondered who or what exactly those who believe that God literally made Roger and us in only days think a chimpanzee is: an intelligently designed near-intelligence; an artful almost-us; an animate allegory, perhaps, like Dr. Tulp's satyr.

I have, during this past week, never lied to Roger, about myself or him, in either word or deed. I have even remarked—if only to myself—that my sitting with him like this each day is in many ways no different from an old ape-house zoo visit. Or, for that matter, the somewhat desperate last dash I would make through Uganda's Kibale rain forest in hopes of having that one encounter with his own species that chimps such as Roger have never had.

It is all, in the end, a form of spying, part of an ongoing attempt on our part to catch in the eyes of the sentient non-us glimpses of who or what we seem to remember ourselves once being.

That, I would explain to Roger if I could, is the true rub of those extra neuronal threads of ours: the illusory sense they create of our expulsion from our own biology, from our own primeval animalistic state. A time when the path of all things, including ourselves, was silent and one: as yet undivided and distanced from us by our own ability to speak of and name things.

Almost all creation mythology pivots around that sense of expulsion and the resulting longing it creates for some restorative return: early language employed to describe language's own distancing effects; stories in which our imagined severance from the rest of nature is invariably perpetrated by an animal. Creatures with whom we once lived in harmony and now cage and stare at.

From the Serpent in the Old Testament to the Fox in the more ancient southern Sudanese Nuer creation myth. According to the Nuer, all creatures, including man, originally lived together in harmony in one camp. The trouble began after Fox persuaded Mongoose to throw a club into Elephant's face. This set off a quarrel. The animals separated, each going its own way, living apart and killing each other as they do now.

The stomach, meanwhile, which originally lived on its own in the forest, entered into man, making him hungry, as did the sexual organs, attaching themselves to men and women, causing them to desire one another. Mice, in turn, taught us to propagate, while the elephant is said to have taught us how to pound millet so that we labor to satisfy our hunger, and so on, all the same dynamics behind the biblical fall and expulsion from paradise.

We, I'd like to tell Roger, were never expelled from anywhere. We walked out: those very first upright forays that Dr. Hof was talking about in his cooler of brains that day. The ones that Roger's ancestors never made with ours. Ever longer and more venturesome treks into different environments, exposing a still inchoate brain to the sort of new and alien entanglements of which our present-day allotment of spindle cells and all the stories we've woven with them over time are both the extant and ever-expanding archives.

Four thirty-five A.M. Roger has seemingly lost track of himself and his doings. His carefully cupped hands keep coming undone, the right one loosely shoving whatever it is he thinks that he's got hold of into the left hand, which he then lets flop over, palm up, against the cement floor beside him. He's been carrying on in this somewhat listless manner for a few minutes. I'm trying to catch his eye, but he is staring straight past me, still in a trance.

Four thirty-nine A.M. Roger has suddenly straightened up again, aware, it seems, of the spillage around him. He's resuming the air piling now, and with his former, caring, two-handed approach, but at what appears to be a slightly faster and more urgent pace, his eyes blinking, as though to the rhythm of some observed action or recalled sound.

I remember sitting up in my Sioux City motel room that second night, blinking back the vacuity of Kirk Cameron's eyes, my quest to find Ripley having apparently come to a sudden and perversely premature dead end. And then I caught hold of myself, cleared Cameron and "The Way of the Master" off my computer screen, and decided to look up Bam Bam.

I was eventually able to trace him here to the Center for Great Apes, and took down the contact numbers, thinking it a place I might want to visit. I then returned to the list of responses garnered by my original search entry for Cameron's documentary, and with one of those wearily impatient, last-minute perusals one does before shutting the computer down, I clicked on an intriguingly entitled website, wildlifepimps.com.

There, beneath a bright red headline that read "Chimpanzee Carnage at Zoo Nebraska," was a picture of a somewhat crazed-looking Ripley and, opposite him, the Emmy- and two-time Tony Award–winning actress Swoosie Kurtz, dressed in a fetching sleeveless black evening gown and smiling broadly.

A Nebraska native like Johnny Carson, Kurtz, it turns out, had taken up Ripley's cause, having written letters to Ken Schlueter at Zoo Nebraska as well as to the director of the Nebraska Department of Tourism, and one to Dave Heineman, the governor of Nebraska, appealing to them for Ripley's immediate release from the "woefully inadequate" facility to which he'd been dispatched: Savanahland Educational Park, near someplace called Lee's Summit, Missouri, a small town, I soon determined, just south of Kansas City, only a couple of hours south of me. Kurtz concludes her appeal with a request that Ripley be allowed to spend the rest of his days with some of his surviving family members, who are currently being kept at the St. Louis Zoo, on Missouri's eastern border.

But my renewed sense of purpose notwithstanding, I knew even as I was heading toward Kansas City the following morning that it was not going to be easy gaining an audience with Ripley. A quick visit to Savanahland's website that night had revealed for one that it, too, was a seasonal facility not scheduled to open until mid-April, still weeks away. As for the chances of a personal off-season tour for an outsider such as myself, showing up one day out of the blue, I was beginning to have serious doubts, especially given the recent Swoosie Kurtz campaign on

Ripley's behalf and the less-than-flattering characterization of his new home offered by wildlifepimps.com.

"Savanahland Educational Park," it began, "is a deceptively named facility that breeds and buys exotic animals, tears baby animals away from their mothers so that they can be hand-raised, and subjects animals, including babies, to the stress of being exhibited at public events. . . . Savanahland is nothing more than a roadside zoo that blatantly exploits exotic animals."

Ripley's new home state of Missouri is, in fact, the virtual nexus of the nation's vast market for rare and exotic species. Four times each year, everyone from roadside-zoo and traveling-circus owners, to big-game-hunt ranch owners, to exotic and rare-species breeders and brokers from all across the United States gather at the Lolli Brothers Alternative Livestock and Bird Sale, the country's largest exotic animal auction, in Macon, Missouri, not far outside Mark Twain's hometown of Hannibal.

There one can buy, as Lolli Brothers advertises, everything "from Apes to Zebras," including African lions (bred like pet-shop puppies in captivity and sold for as little as $250), Siberian tiger cubs for about $3,000 a pair, two-toed sloths for $1,500, nilgai antelopes at $1,000, numerous species of monkeys and primates from macaques starting at about $2,500 each to baby chimps at about $40,000 each. Black bear cubs fetch just $395, but are highly coveted commodities, as their value only increases long after their zoo days are done: their claws, rendered jewelry; their skins, rugs; their flesh, restaurant meat; their paws, valuable exports to Asia (where they're regarded as delicacies). Bear gall-bladders, however, are the most precious items of all, prized by Koreans as aphrodisiacs and medicinal aids, and garnering their smugglers as much as $2,000 each.

Many of these animals (the auction also features an extensive selection of taxidermy) are either recycled seasonal outcasts of the nation's big corporate-sponsored wildlife theme parks, or the unwanted surpluses of accredited major metropolitan zoos across the country. Facilities that—their dreamy, real-life dioramas and messages of conservation and species preservation notwithstanding—regularly unload their older animals to nonaccredited roadside facilities such as Zoo Nebraska or Savanahland to make room for more crowd-pleasing younger animals and cuddly newborns.

The dark underbelly of modern-day zoo-keeping, the exotic-animals trade is, by and large, licensed and legal and, like the right to bear arms in the United States, just as staunchly defended. There is even a digest of the industry, known as the *Animal Finders' Guide.* Published eighteen times a year, the guide typically runs ads for more than 150 species of mammals, birds, and reptiles. It informs readers about upcoming auctions and shows; contains feature stories along the lines of "Do Bobcats Make Good Pets?" and "Suggestions on Raising Servals"; prints letters to the editor decrying the efforts of animal rights activists and lawmakers to restrict exotic-animal ownership; and runs frequent editorials by the publication's founder, Patrick Hoctor, impassioned screeds that would be at home in the pages of any libertarian or anarchist manifesto.

"One by one," Hoctor once wrote about the country's state fish and game departments, "compound by compound, county by county, state by state, they are attacking your brothers and sisters in this business. We better learn to stand side by side and defend one another or, someday, there will be no private ownership of animals in this country!"

A few minutes outside the grounds of Savanahland—set inside a wide-open expanse of manicured parkland with a huge man-made lake—I pulled over and called Bex on my cell phone to let her know that I was about to go in. I told her that if she didn't hear from me in the next couple of hours, she should call the police. I said I was having dark visions of being kidnapped, chloroformed, and taxidermed, rendered a prized specialty item for an upcoming Lolli Brothers auction.

Driving a newly paved, two-lane road around the southern end of Savanahland's lake, I kept repeating to myself the warning issued by wildlifepimps.com about keeping any pleas on Ripley's behalf "polite and thoughtful."

"Rudeness and accusations," they warn, "will not help Ripley's situation." Nor mine, I told myself. Not so long ago Ripley would have been just one more anonymous cast-off of the seedy carnival sideshow world. Now he's a cause célèbre of movie stars. The watchdogs and the watched of this world are all well aware of each other by now. One can't even show up at a pokey little place such as Savanahland on an off-season morning in March and ask to see a chimpanzee without instantly arousing suspicion. This seemed to me a truly hopeful development for the human race as a whole and yet, for my own immediate purposes, petrifying.

I followed the road around to Savanahland's front gates. There was a young boy, no older than six or seven, idling about before a large grassy enclosure containing some zebras. I got out of the car and took a quick look around.

The facility, some eighty acres in all, slopes gently away from the front gate in an ongoing series of enclosures inside of which I could see antelopes, camels, hyenas, and a huge warthog. Farther down the hill to my right was a telltale domelike structure with makeshift vine swings and an attached cinder-block housing unit not unlike the ones at the Center for Great Apes. Ripley, I knew then, had to be down there somewhere.

I walked over and introduced myself to the boy, asked him if he lived at Savanahland. He nodded and pointed way into the distance at a brick house with a wraparound porch set along the very road I'd come on.

"And do you know Ripley?" I asked, at a complete loss for conversation.

He nodded.

"And how is Ripley?"

"He loves it here."

I thought for a moment about having the boy show me around. But not knowing who might be out on the grounds, I decided to play it safe and asked him instead if there was someone on hand who could give me a quick tour.

He nodded again.

"I'll go get my grandpa," he said, then ran off down the road in the direction of the brick house.

I waited by that entrance gate for at least another half hour, alternately staring down at Ripley's dome and the distant brick house up the road, waiting for some sign of activity. Midway between those two antipodes, Savanahland's array of displaced beasts seemed to all turn and stare at once, subsuming me into their collective bewilderment.

What, I wondered, does a hyena or an antelope make of a small patch of grass in western Missouri? Something must seem different to them, amiss. Even the familiar, seamless drift of an aquarium fish's day, after all, keeps bringing them back around to bump their nose against the glass.

Leave now, I kept telling myself, becoming more convinced the longer I stood there that something nefarious was indeed being cooked up for me—a notion made all the more absurd by the fact that in another three weeks I could show up at that very gate as a typical paying customer and have all the time I wanted with Ripley.

Just then I noticed a small golf cart approaching from the

vicinity of the brick house. I stood by, watching it come toward me. A tall, lean, sinewy gentleman in jeans, a denim work shirt, and a cowboy hat was driving.

The cart stopped right in front of me. I nodded. The driver nodded back. He looked, well, impatient, wary. I'm not sure of this, but I believe he was shaking his head before I'd even started talking.

"I'm real busy," he said, cutting me off just a couple of words into my roadside-zoo-book spiel.

"I don't need much time. It's just that I've driven quite a ways, and I was—"

"Sorry," he said, turning the wheel. "Too much to do." And then he sped away.

I remained there a moment before getting in my car and driving off, staring back down the hill toward Ripley's place, wondering, as I had so many nights back in Brooklyn, what was going through Ripley's mind at that very moment, wondering whether he will ever get to see his family again.

I decided to drive due east that day, straight to the other side of Missouri. Not to meet Ripley's family, but to visit yet another facility along the lines of Savanahland that I'd read about in the course of tracking down Ripley. A place called the Missouri Primate Foundation, outside the town of Festus, forty-five miles south of St. Louis. Nothing like a couple of near misses to steel one's resolve.

Originally known as "Chimp Party," the Missouri Primate Foundation presents itself as a sanctuary for captive chimpanzees—outcasts of zoos, research labs, and the entertainment industry. It is therefore able to gain tax-exempt status, all the while breeding and selling baby chimps as either pets or future entertainers, as well as renting out its own chimpanzees for such things as kids' birthday parties, television commercials, and promotional videos. At the time of my visit, the Missouri Primate Foundation's website still featured a photo of chimps dressed up in diapers and Santa's caps against a quilted backdrop of waving stars and stripes.

Chimp Party, I also learned, had a calamitous breakout incident of its own in 2001. It seems to come with the territory. According to local newspaper accounts, the facility's co-owner, Connie Casey, whose husband, Mike, was on the road that day with some of their chimps making a TV commercial, had failed to adequately secure one of the cages, and three of their chimps soon found themselves roaming the back roads of Festus, a rural, woodsy enclave of small clapboard houses with fenced-in yards.

The chimps ended up in the yard of a neighbor whose seventeen-year-old son was just arriving home in a pickup truck with two friends as Connie Casey was madly trying to rein the animals in. The seventeen-year-old claimed the chimps were threatening him and his friends, surrounding the truck, preventing them from getting out. According to neighbors, many of whom knew these very chimps, having had them over to their houses for their children's birthday parties, the chimps were merely out walking around, not threatening anyone.

The boys eventually made their way into the house. Connie Casey, meanwhile, had managed to get one tranquilizer dart into the oldest of the chimps, the twenty-eight-year-old Suzy. It was then—according to a number of neighbors and some local contractors who'd been working at the Caseys' compound when the breakout occurred and were helping to recapture the chimps—that the seventeen-year-old emerged from his house with a shotgun.

With two of the chimps a safe distance away, the youth set his sights on Suzy, nearly unconscious by then, druggily picking flowers at the end of the driveway. Against the pleas of Casey and her helpers, he shot Suzy. When the other chimps gathered beside their mortally wounded companion, he threatened to kill them as well, but Casey and the contractors gathered around the chimps and managed to shield them with their bodies.

I made it from Savanahland to Festus in just over three and a half hours, pulling up at about three o'clock that afternoon before the locked front gate of the Caseys' compound and the by now familiar tableau of exiled exotics, animals too inured to their confines to even startle.

Three baby chimps were twirling and tumbling about in a party-colored painted pen. A very curious emu strutted back and forth on the far side of the fence, eyeballing me. Down a slight hill from where I was standing, an old boxer began to waddle its way in my direction from the front porch of a rather elaborate log-cabin-style home. On the porch I could make out four large plastic chimps in the "Hear No Evil, See No Evil, Speak No Evil" poses, the fourth one with its hands held over its crotch above the words "Have No Fun." From the far back of the compound, the sudden clamor of captive chimpanzees rose on the afternoon air.

I waited at the gate awhile, then decided to try Chimp Party's phone number. I got a recording and hung up. After another ten minutes or so, with still no sign of my own species, I phoned again and left a message. I said that I was at the front gate, going on to explain that I was from out of town, had heard about Chimp Party, happened to be passing through, and was hoping to see the place and gather some stories for a book I was writing.

Within moments I saw the front door of the log-cabin house opening. A middle-aged woman, dressed in blue jeans and a flowered denim shirt, stepped out and started up the hill in my direction. She arrived at the other side of the gate, introduced herself as Connie Casey, and before I could utter a word, she told me in a very polite, nearly apologetic tone that I needed to go speak with her husband, Mike.

"He's right over there," she said, pointing across a wide wooded valley to the far side of their animal compound where a lone brick ranch house sat on a grassy hilltop.

Following her directions, I drove half a mile back along the road I'd come in on, took the first right, and then made my way up a winding mountain road that led me directly to the ranch house. Looking back across the valley, I could see now the full extent of the Casey chimpanzee compound: a towering, brand-new cement and steel housing unit with an expansive outdoor enclosure filled with the requisite makeshift vines, strewn toys, and tire swings.

I pulled into Mike Casey's driveway, hopped out, and immediately spotted a large, square-shouldered man with a substantial paunch seated in a folding chair atop the front steps. I went straight up the walkway to him, extended a hand, and introduced myself, immediately apologizing for just dropping in on him in this way.

"Look," he said, standing now, his face going into a pained wince, instantly accentuating the disfigured, restitched bulge of his nose, the result—I instantly suspected and it would later be confirmed by a worker I'd meet at Chimp Haven outside Shreveport, Louisiana, who knew of Mike Casey and his business—of a very bad chimpanzee bite.

"If you're one of these A.R. people pretending to be something else, I'm telling you right now, you and me are gonna have big trouble."

I assured him that I had no particular agenda, that I wanted only to hear stories about human interactions with chimps, and that I would love to get the chance to meet some of his.

"I have nothing really against animal rights people," he went on. "They have their point of view, and I respect that. It's just that they're so damned dogmatic about it."

I nodded.

"Here's the deal," he said. "I've got a real sick father inside who needs my attention. Would you mind coming back later this afternoon? Let's say at around five o'clock?"

I gave Mike Casey my cell phone number, told him to call me whenever he was ready, then drove the four miles or so back out to the stretch of fast-food joints and strip malls that constitute downtown Festus. I found myself a little picnic bench there at the far end of a gas station parking lot and sat down to read about what ultimately became of the Temerlins' chimpanzee daughter, Lucy.

That part of the story, it turns out, isn't to be found in *Growing Up Human*. I had skipped ahead to the memoir's final chapter in my Sioux City motel room the previous night. Dr. Temerlin writes that after ten years with Lucy—during which he "had explored the deepest depths of the psychobiological basis of being human, for here was Lucy, biologically a chimpanzee to be sure, but psychologically able to live healthily and happily as a human being"—he and Jane had finally decided that the two of them now wanted "more freedom to live a normal life."

He goes on to contemplate the various alternatives for what to do with Lucy, a nearly schizophrenic series of musings that begins with Temerlin flatly stating that although Lucy greatly enriched his family's life and their growth as people, their raising her "was a horrible thing to do."

Then, by way of underscoring just how cruel it would be to now put her into either a zoo or a large colony of former captive chimpanzees, Temerlin offers a two-page synopsis of Lucy's previous day, described as a "typical Lucy Temerlin day." The account somehow winds up being more chilling than any of the previously recounted perversions of this animal's ten-year stint as a human being.

She awakened, we're told, at 7:00 A.M. after eight hours of sleep "in a king-sized bed on a Simmons Beautyrest mattress" alongside Jane. (Dr. Temerlin had already explained in an earlier chapter that after his and Jane's twenty years of marriage, Lucy and Jane had taken to sleeping together and he alone in a separate room because Lucy had become too jealous of his and Jane's lovemaking.)

Upon waking, Lucy sleepily walked into the living room, sat on the family's "Danish modern sofa," and, after a cup of coffee, made a circular nest of sofa cushions on the floor. For the next half hour or so she lolled about, looking at *Time, Newsweek,* and *National Geographic,* then repaired to the breakfast table to eat a bowl of oatmeal topped with raisins and beef protein powder, along with a glass of grape Tang.

After an hour and a half of playtime by herself in her room, Lucy met with two American Sign Language specialists for a two-hour language lesson during which Lucy initiated many of the conversations and broke off at one point to go into the kitchen and fill the kettle with water to make everyone cups of tea. As Dr. Temerlin found himself with no noontime psychotherapy patients in his home office that day, he decided to have lunch with Lucy, she having her usual two four-minute soft-boiled eggs, half a pint of peach yogurt, and an orange.

The afternoon hours Lucy spent alone in her room sleeping and playing and staring out the window at the countryside. When Jane came home in the evening, she, Dr. Temerlin, and Lucy all had gin and tonics together. (The Temerlins' son, Steven, was away at college at the time.) During the second round of drinks, Lucy, impatient for dinner, went to the fridge and helped herself to a carton of yogurt, some leftover pot roast, a carrot, half a carton of defrosted frozen strawberries, and some bites out of a head of lettuce. She then curled up on the living room sofa under her blanket and went to sleep.

One could be forgiven for suspecting Dr. Temerlin of a bit of embellishment in all of this. And yet no less an authority on, and studious observer of, chimpanzees than Jane Goodall wrote a strikingly similar account of Lucy, having visited the Temerlins in the course of a lecture circuit stop at the University of Oklahoma in 1972.

"Lucy . . . went into the kitchen," Goodall writes. "She opened two cupboards, taking a glass from one and a bottle of gin from the other. She opened the refrigerator, extracted a bottle of tonic, then closed the door with a careful and deliberate action as though it were a pleasurable thing to do. After neatly taking the cap from the tonic with her teeth, she mixed herself a strong drink. She came back into the living room, drink in hand, and turned on the television. After scanning through the channels and finding nothing that suited her taste, she turned it off and then lounged in an easy chair with a magazine and her gin and tonic. It was remarkable."

Later, Goodall recounts an extraordinary scene of Lucy talking to herself in sign language while looking through a magazine: "Lucy . . . repeatedly signed to herself as she turned the pages. Jane Temerlin translated for me. 'Blue' signed Lucy, gazing at a picture of a woman in a blue dress; 'that dog' she proclaimed, turning to a picture of a toy poodle. And so on, until she reached the end. She made no mistakes, she only signed about things on some of the pages, and she was utterly absorbed, paying absolutely no attention to either Jane or me. At the end Jane signed 'Whose magazine?' and Lucy replied 'Mine, Lucy's.'"

The thought of putting such an individual into a chimpanzee colony, Dr. Temerlin writes, "brings to mind the Jewish intellectuals of Germany who were honored citizens of the most culturally and scientifically advanced nation in Europe one day, and found themselves without friends, property, or personhood the next, as they were herded behind the barbed wire of the concentration camp. Human-raised chimpanzees have been integrated into colonies of chimpanzees before, but it has never been done with a chimpanzee who has been with humans exclusively or for so long. . . . [T]he chimpanzee experiences much fear, terror, and pain before becoming a chimp among chimps. Often chimpanzee madness results, even with the best of gradual initiation rites."

Dr. Temerlin considered a number of other alternatives, including various lines of research he felt would be beneficial to both science and Lucy's welfare: having Lucy impregnated, for example, with semen from a colonized chimpanzee to determine whether she would mother the baby instinctually or if such behavior must be learned; or attempting to mate Lucy with a male chimp; or giving her a baby chimp of her own to rear to see how that relationship would evolve and whether Lucy would try to communicate with her adopted child using the natural sounds and gestures of a wild chimpanzee or the American Sign Language she had learned, or perhaps some combination of the two.

Dr. Temerlin again promised a number of sequels to *Growing Up Human,* to be written by him or Jane, or both, so that we might learn of their ultimate decision about Lucy and "finally have an ending."

"I was raised in the romantic tradition," he wrote in his book's final paragraph, "and I like books to have happy endings. If they do not have happy endings they should have tragic endings. I hate books which have no ending—like this one."

The story of Lucy's end, it turns out, would first emerge in a series of articles published in *Smithsonian* and in *Reader's Digest* in the 1980s. They were written by Janis Carter, a graduate student at the University of Oklahoma who, in the course of working for the Temerlins as both a babysitter and cage cleaner, had gotten to be friendly with Lucy and learned to communicate with her in sign language. Carter would soon find herself caught up in the throes of the Temerlins' next experiment with Lucy: a curious, if consistently contorted, decision to try to transform their darling, virginal, gin-and-tonic-swilling daughter back into a wild chimpanzee.

The word "back" is, of course, not entirely accurate as Lucy, like Roger, was born in captivity, but the Temerlins had heard about a project in Gambia, on the West Coast of Africa, devoted to trying to habituate captive chimpanzees to the wilderness and decided this would be the ideal alternative.

In the late summer of 1977, they and Janis Carter flew together to Gambia along with two wooden crates, one holding Lucy, the other, Marianne, another captive-born chimp, a young female who had recently become a friend of Lucy's at the University of Oklahoma.

The Temerlins stayed in Africa for only a few days. The plan was for Carter to accompany Lucy and Marianne to a temporary holding facility in a small forest reserve near Banjul, the capital of Gambia, to help Lucy get acclimated to her new environment. After three weeks, Carter also was to return home to the States, and the project's caretakers would assume responsibility for Lucy's gradual transition to a life in the jungles of neighboring Senegal.

Lucy, however, immediately became deeply depressed and came down with a number of illnesses, and Carter soon found herself extending her stay for longer and longer periods. She became increasingly concerned about her charge's physical and mental health and, once in Senegal, about the ever-present threat of territorial attacks from wild chimpanzees in the region.

In the end, Carter wound up staying at the reserve outside Banjul for three years, taking on seven other chimps in that time. Then, in the spring of 1979, she moved all nine of her charges two hundred miles inland, along the Gambia River, to one of the five Baboon Islands there, thus setting in motion one of the odder episodes ever recorded in the history of inter-species relationships.

Gambia's indigenous chimpanzee population had been wiped out by the early 1900s, so there was no threat of territo-rial battles in the former captive chimps' new habitat. Mostly flat, narrow landmasses of tall gallery forest with occasional patches of swamp and savanna, the Baboon Islands are host to a number of primate species, the Guinea baboon for which they're named being the most plentiful, along with a wide assort-ment of other species, including anteaters, servals, otters, hippos, Nile crocodiles, a variety of antelopes, and numerous species of snakes and birds; all in all, an ideal niche for Carter's chimp exiles to try to fill.

Still, to facilitate their transition back to nature, Carter resorted to a radical gesture. She had a group of British comman-dos who were training on the island build for her a big wire enclosure. She then took her few possessions, moved into the enclosure, and locked the chimps out. She would become, in effect, the captive that her charges once were so they might dis-cover the free, wild beasts they were never allowed to be.

"From the beginning," she wrote, "the chimps would have to accept that I alone lived in a cage."

Carter, especially at the beginning, did make frequent instructive forays into the surrounding jungle, climbing trees and foraging for food, eating everything from figs to ants, "living," she wrote, "more as a chimpanzee than as a human." She even built herself a treetop platform to sleep on at night by way of encouraging the chimps to build their own nests. And for the most part they all began to follow suit, climbing trees, gathering their own food, drinking water from the river, making treetop nests.

All but for the Simmons Beautyrest queen Lucy. The seven chimps Carter had acquired in the reserve outside Banjul were all wild-born and so had some survival skills. Marianne, meanwhile, had been in the company of other chimps for much of her life in captivity and was able to integrate with her companions and imitate what they were doing. The wholly humanized, language-wielding Lucy, however, approached matters quite differently.

As the largest of the nine chimps on the island and the only one who could converse with Carter, Lucy was yet another evolutionary anomaly that only we humans could fashion: the dominant chimp of her group and yet the one least capable of surviving on her own. She insisted on drinking water as Carter did, from a bottle and not from the river. While the other chimps would be at the top of a baobob tree foraging for food, Lucy would steadfastly refuse to climb, positioning herself instead at the base of the tree and waiting for edible morsels to fall.

Carter writes of one instance when Lucy asked her in sign language for help getting food from a tree. Carter tried to show her a quick way up the tree from an adjacent one, but Lucy took Carter by the hand, put that hand against the tree trunk, and then signed, "More food. Janis go."

Carter eventually decided to retreat to her enclosure, stop all communication with Lucy, and leave her to find food on her own. A standoff ensued, Lucy positioning herself outside Carter's cage, refusing to move, growing more and more emaciated. She'd whine and pluck her hair out and occasionally sign: "Food . . . drink . . . Janis come out . . . Lucy's hurt." When Carter tried to shoo her away, Lucy would go a short distance off and then slowly make her way back to the side of the cage again.

This went on for months, Carter reports, and then one day she and Lucy, exhausted from their struggles, fell asleep beside one another. When Carter awoke, she found Lucy sitting up outside, offering Carter a leaf through the bars of the enclosure. Carter ate some and gave the rest to Lucy, and from that point on, Carter says, Lucy finally began to fend for herself, gradually regaining her health and strength.

In 1985, six years after first setting up her Baboon Islands camp, Carter decided it was time to leave the chimps to their own devices. Lucy had by then seemingly made a successful transition to her new surroundings. She even adopted an orphaned baby male chimpanzee and managed to overcome her grief when her adopted son died of a stomach parasite three years later. She also survived her own near fatal bout of hookworm and, by the time of Carter's departure, was in good physical health and showing positive signs of social interactions with the other chimps.

And yet for Lucy—as Carter was about to learn in the course of a subsequent visit to the island by boat from her new base camp downriver—the boundary between her former and her rightful, natural place in the world would remain forever contentious and confused.

There is a photograph from that visit of Carter's, one almost too fraught to look at. It was taken in 1986, some six months after Carter's initial departure from the island. Carter has just pulled her boat onshore, and Lucy—always the first to greet any human visitor to the island—has rushed out of the jungle to her old friend's side.

The two of them sit clutching one another by the waters of the Gambia River, a wall of jungle rising behind them, each of them outcasts of their original selves; like two primates, you might say, passing in the night: Carter, the classic American sub-

urban girl, looking more attuned now to jungle living than her suburban-raised, humanized chimp counterpart; Lucy's head bowed against Carter's chest as though in mortification, her long left hand furled against her chin, beneath a mournful, downcast brow.

Carter had brought with her that day some of Lucy's possessions from her past life: pens and paper, books, a doll, a hat, and a mirror. Lucy is said to have given them only a cursory look before standing, looking back at Carter, and then walking off into the jungle.

A year later, Lucy's skeleton, minus the hands and feet, would be found on the grounds of Carter's former camp, near the site of her old wire enclosure. There were no indications of her hav-ing suffered a fall or an attack from another animal.

The most likely scenario of her end, given the missing hands and feet and skin, is that Lucy—still drawn, like Roger, more to people than to members of his own species—unwittingly approached in greeting a group of poachers, who readily seized upon their overeager prey.

Mike Casey didn't call me back that day until about five thirty. He said he was still tied up, asked if I could come by in another hour. I told him fine. It only occurred to me later that whatever else he might have been up to that afternoon, he'd been spending a good portion of it Googling me, doing background checks, trying to confirm whether I was, in fact, one of those "A.R. people."

I couldn't quite construe what from my publishing past—a memoir about the log cabin in Canada; one about being disguised as a surgeon to witness the harvesting of a human heart; and a novel narrated by a dying dog—might possibly set off any alarms in Mike Casey's head.

Still, driving back toward his house that evening, I kept having the same dark fantasies I had while waiting at the gates to Savanahland, picturing Casey waiting in that chair by the front door, but this time with a shotgun. Or once I was inside his house, his slipping something into my coffee, torturing me for a confession, and then tossing me, like some animate rope toy, into one of his chimps' enclosures.

Here I was, roaming around the middle of the country, visiting the likes of Savanahland and Chimp Party, merely to spy again. To spy, in this instance, on what I thought was an out-moded way of keeping and viewing wild animals, one as near to extinction as a number of the animals being so kept, and yet was now beginning to fear might be another prefigurement of the wild's only remaining future: a world of variously sized and shaped wildlife theme parks, the respective inhabitants preserved for viewing or shooting or both.

It was nearly dark by the time I pulled back into Mike Casey's driveway. The front porch chair was empty. Lights were on everywhere inside, silhouettes shifting about as I started up the walkway and knocked on the front door. Connie Casey answered and invited me into what was essentially one big rec-tangular room, like an outsized house trailer.

To the left, behind a mini wood-balustrade partition, was the kitchen area. The rest was all living room: a dimly lit, shag-carpeted, faux-wood-paneled array of leather sofas and chairs; a shiny glass coffee table; shelves of chimp figurines; and what appeared to be a stone fireplace that had since been converted to house a massive home entertainment unit featuring a giant, big-screen television and standing speakers on either side. To the far right, a hallway led to the house's remaining rooms.

I was led into the kitchen. Mike Casey was seated there at one of those chunky, wooden, homesteader-style table-and-chair sets with the requisite wagon-wheel light fixture above. His hands were folded on the table before him. Connie Casey offered me a cup of coffee.

"So," Mike Casey began, "tell me about harvesting a heart. That sounds amazing."

I knew right then it would be some time before we'd even get around to the subject of chimpanzees. When we finally did, I first asked if I might pay a visit to some of the Caseys' twenty-three chimps.

"No," Mike Casey said. "It's too late. They're all settling in for the night. Perhaps another time."

I pulled my tape recorder from my sports coat pocket and placed it on the table. Mike Casey shook his head.

"We aren't at that stage in our relationship yet."

When I took out my notebook to write some things down, I got another big, nose-crinkling wince.

"I wish you wouldn't."

With all that settled, I was soon being shown a number of photo albums, endless shots, elaborately annotated, of Kimmy, Kenzy, Conner, and Kirby, chimps the Caseys had raised as their own children. There were pictures of them eating at the very table where we were sitting; shots of them playing with the Caseys' twin grandchildren, and with their old pet boxer, the one that had waddled up to greet me earlier in the day at the front gate.

There was, as well, a series of star shots: Kenzy with wrestler Hulk Hogan, and with the actor/comedian John Leguizamo; pictures of Mike Casey's favorite chimp son, Kirby, with the singer Sheryl Crow on the now defunct *Michael Moore Show.*

"Kirby! My Kirby Do!" Casey kept cooing as he flipped from one shot to the next. "Kirby-Do-Doodle! My doodle-bug!"—the same stream of baby talk he'd be sounding an hour later as we all sat on the living room sofa together, watching on the fireplace entertainment center *Kirby's Tooth Fairy Tales,* a half-hour-long promotional video made for a local dentist, starring Kirby as the ideal patient and practitioner of sound dental hygiene.

"We always took showers together when he was growing up," Mike Casey told me, "and brushing his teeth was his favorite part."

Casey was on the road with Kirby, he told me, filming a

commercial, the day that Suzy and the two other chimps escaped the compound. The room went silent when I first brought it up. I could see that Mike Casey was fighting back tears. Then his fist hit the kitchen table, and he looked straight at me.

"I'd have shot that bastard kid if I were there," he said. "He and his friends were always going around saying how they were going to nail one of them chimps. That kid should be in jail."

"It was horrible," Connie Casey said. "I watched him murder one of my own family."

That Suzy's death was in any way a consequence of her unnatural confinement seemed never to have occurred to the Caseys. The fault in their eyes, the failure of imagination, lay with those who aren't able to see just how sophisticated, how truly like us, chimps are—the very point, strangely enough, that "A.R people" stress on behalf of protecting chimps from places such as Chimp Party.

In fact, the Caseys, it soon occurred to me, could be considered the more forward-thinking: another version of the Temerlins but without the psychobabble or pretense of science. Mike and Connie Casey had either never considered the concept of the chimpanzees' rightful, original place in the wild, or they considered that notion entirely retrograde. Chimps to them are little people, and what they, the Caseys, do with chimps only underscores that fact. It dignifies and advances them by accentuating their closeness to us.

"The children's birthday parties we take them to," Mike Casey said to me at one point, his hand slapping the table again, "are just as enriching and educational for the chimps as they are for the children."

I thought back to some comments I'd been reading earlier that very afternoon by none other than the original owner of the Temerlins' Lucy, a woman named Mae Noell, the late proprietor of a place called Chimp Farm in Tarpon Springs, Florida, long one of the country's largest and most notorious roadside zoos and chimp-breeding facilities, shut down in 1999 by the U.S. Department of Agriculture after repeatedly failing inspections.

Dr. Temerlin, it seems, not only wrote a book without an ending, but also omitted, or purposely fudged, a number of details about his "darling daughter's" beginnings as well. Lucy, it turns out, was born into a large group of carnival chimpanzees raised at Chimp Farm by Mae Noell and her husband, Bob, former vaudeville stage actors who, from 1940 to the early 1970s, also operated an immensely popular animal act known as "Noell's Ark Gorilla Show."

Traveling to small towns up and down the eastern seaboard, the show featured boxing and wrestling matches between a volunteer from the crowd and one of the Noells' chimps. The chimp would be muzzled, harnessed, and fitted with gloves and tennis shoes to avoid any serious injury to its opponent. Still, there was never any doubt about the outcome.

In fact, the length of any bout would invariably be determined by the timorousness or machismo of the human involved. The more of the latter, the briefer the match, the town's biggest and most aggressive tough guys being the ones most readily dispatched with one swinging chimp leg kick, or a powerful swipe of a forearm, once fearsome he-men reduced in a moment to whimpering children.

According to Mae Noell, who died back in October 2000, ten years after her husband, she originally sold Lucy to William Lemmon, a researcher at the Institute for Primate Studies in Norman, Oklahoma, with the understanding that Lucy would be used for only noninvasive research and then be returned to Chimp Farm after his experiment was over. Lemmon instead decided to give Lucy to his secretary, Jane Temerlin.

Over breakfast one morning in a Tarpon Springs diner back in the early 1990s, Noell spoke about her life with chimpanzees with writer Dale Peterson, coauthor with Jane Goodall of the book *Visions of Caliban: On Chimpanzees and People.*

A self-described Christian fundamentalist, Noell told Peterson that her experiences with chimps had nevertheless left her at odds with her fellow Christians on the subject of evolution and our kinship with apes.

"This critter is a very close cousin, *very* close cousin," she explained. "He is a human being except for his ability to talk and understand morals. He can't understand morals and the Bible . . . but he is a very close cousin. The truth is he's got the same number and type of teeth that we've got, same muscles, same bones, and they've recently found they've got the same blood types. How much closer can you get? . . . I really feel they are people—of a lower grade. And I've been criticized for that. Now the way I answer some of these Bible people: We know that the Lord made two people, a man and a woman. They had two children, two sons. One of them killed the other. The murderer, according to the Bible, was sent out into the wilderness and found himself a wife! Think about it! That's all I'm going to say. It's something to think about, you know. It ties in with evolution."

(Oddly enough, I once heard the very same Cain-and-Abel theory espoused by a Mohawk Indian chief as an explanation for why the white man's body is covered with so much hair compared to the Indian's.)

Mae Noell went on to tell Dale Peterson that Lucy was rightfully hers, that she still had in her possession Dr. Lemmon's promise, written on Institute for Primate Studies stationery, that Lucy would be returned to Chimp Farm once experiments with her had been completed. As for the Temerlins' decision to release Lucy into the wilds of Gambia, Noell was no less forthcoming.

"Most cruel damn thing that could have been done to anything," she told Peterson. "You're sitting here now, at a table. And she sat at a table. You're wearing clothes. She wore clothes. You're drinking warm coffee, you're eating hot food already prepared for you. How would it be to take all your clothes off and go out into that tree? There's nothing but trees around here, and I've got to figure out what I can eat and how I can cover my body so I don't freeze to death or get rained on?"

From far across the valley between the Caseys' two houses, one shrill chimp scream sounded. Mike Casey turned to me and smiled.

"That's the Kirby-Doodle right now! Little doodlebug."

It was well past eight in the evening, Mike Casey standing to put on another video, when I finally made up something about a dinner engagement with an old friend in St. Louis and began gathering my belongings.

As Casey was walking me out to my car, I decided to mention the most frequent complaint leveled against Chimp Party and the Missouri Primate Foundation: that while they do adopt and take good care of many orphaned and outcast former research-lab and roadside-zoo chimpanzees, they also breed baby chimps for sale as pets, often advertising in places such as the *Animal Finders' Guide,* thus producing more future orphaned outcasts.

"First of all," he said, stopping along the front walk, "we don't use that word 'pet.' They are part of the family. We also do extensive background checks on the people we sell a chimp to, in order to make sure they're not going to be used for the wrong reasons."

Casey stopped again at the driveway's edge. I turned to shake his hand. He didn't seem to notice.

"I'm so sick of hearing about how I'm exploiting these animals. To hell with those A.R. people for always foisting their views and their definitions of things on everyone else."

I got in my car. Mike Casey came around to the driver's-side window. I opened it.

"Look," he said, his nose once more in a wince. "They have their idea of sanctuary, and I have mine. Everyone has their own idea of sanctuary."

Faster and faster now Roger is piling his air. I tried waving my arms at him again. I even stood at one point and made as though I were leaving, figuring that would surely get his attention. But nothing has deterred him, not even another chimp scream sounding moments ago from a far-off enclosure, one brief and thankfully noncombustible burst against the prevailing silence.

I have no idea what Roger is up to. It must be something from his past.

And yet it makes no difference any longer that we can't, as the standard warning against anthropomorphizing goes, possibly know what Roger is thinking. Or what a Roger day is like, or a whale's, or an elephant's, or a parrot's.

That is one of the peculiar things about this moment we've arrived at with the animals. We've come to know enough now about the shared biological underpinnings of so many of those brains in Dr. Hof's cooler that somehow the question of what Roger's or another animal's day might be like has become wholly incidental to the fact that they clearly have days, too, and deeply woundable ones.

Science has obviated anthropomorphism—the crime of projecting our stories upon the animals—by, of all things, repeatedly pointing out to us just how uncomfortably close to our stories so many aspects of theirs actually are.

I remember in the course of the daylong, bone-crushing drive a few months ago from Uganda's capital city of Kampala out to Queen Elizabeth National Park to research the story about the psychological and emotional breakdown of elephants in the wild, feeling at a complete loss as to how to even proceed with such a premise.

It is one thing, I thought, to have gone into the Peruvian Amazon as I did years ago to write about the deforestation and declining biodiversity in the region; or into the jungles of southern Belize to write about the attempt to save the remaining jaguar population in that country's southern Cockscomb Basin; or out along India's northern border with Nepal to track the numbers of surviving rhinos in that region.

But here I was on the cusp of a whole other kind of investigative wilderness trek. A metaphysical safari, of sorts, my unlikely quarry being to document the collective nervous breakdown of an entire species. To essentially show that we human beings do have the capacity to render even vast wildernesses the equivalent of this fraught and finite room where Roger sits now before me madly piling up his handfuls of air.

I had all sorts of dire dispatches swirling around in my head my first day out in Queen Elizabeth National Park, my driver, Nelson Okello, and I heading to the village of Kyambura at the far southeastern corner of Queen Elizabeth, the reported site of a recent elephant attack. Images of the wild in final revolt: creatures everywhere pushed by us to their limit, turning around now to push, claw, and blindly thrust back; marauding elephant herds; whales beaching themselves en masse all across the world; stories of chimps, too, lashing out at their own ongoing diminishment, invading villages, stealing away with infants, as though in retribution for the years of killing and kidnapping of their own for everything from the bush-meat trade to the entertainment industry.

Attacks on villages such as Kyambura are now occurring all over the elephants' natural range in Africa, India, and Southeast Asia. They have, in fact, become so commonplace that a new statistical category, known as human-elephant conflict, or H.E.C., has been created by elephant researchers to monitor the problem, and each year the numbers have gotten increasingly worse.

Before leaving the States for Uganda, I was told by a United States–based psychologist named Gay Bradshaw, an expert in animal trauma who is writing a book about what is happening to the world's elephants, that in India, where the elephant has long been regarded as a deity, newspaper headlines are now warning people "To Avoid Confrontation, Don't Worship Elephants."

In the Indian state of Jharkhand, she said, near the western border of Bangladesh, 300 people were killed between 2000 and 2004 alone. In the past twelve years, elephants have killed well over 600 people in Assam, a state in northeastern India. Some 265 elephants died in that same period, the majority of them as a result of retaliation by angry villagers who, absent the formal animal trials of yore, have carried on a kind of vigilante justice, using everything from poison-tipped arrows to laced food to exact their revenge. In Africa, meanwhile, reports of human-elephant conflicts appear almost daily, from Zambia to Tanzania, from Uganda to Sierra Leone, where just last year, 300 villagers had been evacuated from their homes because of repeated elephant attacks.

Still, it's not just the increasing number of these incidents but the singular perversity—for want of a less anthropocentric term—of recent elephant aggression that has been causing so much alarm. Since the early 1990s, adolescent elephants in Pilans-berg National Park and Hluhluwe-Umfolozi Game Reserve in South Africa have been raping and killing rhinoceroses, unprece-dented behavior that is, nevertheless, now being reported in a number of reserves in the region.

In 2006, officials in Pilansberg shot three young male ele-phants who were believed to be responsible for raping and lethally assaulting 63 rhinos, as well as attacking people in safari vehicles. Meanwhile, in Addo Elephant National Park, also in South Africa, 90 percent of male elephant deaths are now attrib-utable to other male elephants, compared with a rate of 6 per-cent in more stable elephant communities.

According to accounts I'd read of the incident in the village of Kyambura, a group of elephants came charging out of the nearby forest, destroyed a number of huts, trampled fields of crops, and then fled. People were now said to be afraid to ven-ture outside the village because elephants were guarding the road to and from town, attacking anyone who attempted to pass.

We were still miles from Kyambura that morning, our Land Rover plying Queen Elizabeth's postdawn mists, me sitting in the passenger seat, perusing with binoculars the parkland's wide-open savanna: the serene beauty of the grazing herds of water buffalo and antelopes, the waving tan grasses and gnarled acacia trees at complete odds with the apocalyptic vision of natural dystopia I'd been building in my head. Then Nelson hit the brakes.

I looked up to see a stop sign at a four-way intersection, something of an anomaly in the middle of the wilderness, and yet, given the volume of passenger-packed safari vehicles I'd soon be seeing out in the park each day, not all that surprising.

Nelson was about to pass through when he hit the brakes again and pointed to our right. A pair of baboons stood hunched against a roadside hedgerow, one of them cradling a baby. We held there for a moment watching, and then the male stood and began to stride, bolt upright, across the road, straight toward us. He came directly to my open passenger-side window, then held out his hand to me, palm up.

I had heard of parrots in the Philippines who, having learned the traffic patterns on city streets, carefully arrange the hardest nuts in their diet along the stop lines at intersections and then allow the cars to do their most difficult shell cracking for them. This baboon's scheme, it seemed, was one more rendition of that phenomenon: an animal so acclimated to the prevalence of safari traffic in the park, he'd figured he could just as readily feed his family from that source as any other.

Neither Nelson nor I had any food to offer him, and I soon found myself in the ridiculous position of gesturing apologetically to a monkey. I remember his head tilting at my own plaintively upturned palms, then looking back at me with such earnest, pout-lipped entreaty that I began reaching into my pockets for change, as though somewhere off beyond those roadside hedges there was a bustling baboon city with bars, gambling parlors, dance halls, and brothels right out of my apocalyptic vision.

Kyambura looked, upon our arrival, much like every other small Ugandan farming community I'd passed. Lush fields of banana trees, millet, and maize framed a small town center of pastel-colored single-story cement buildings with corrugated-tin roofs. People sat on stoops out front in the available shade. Bicyclers bore preposterously outsized loads of bananas, firewood, and five-gallon water jugs on their fenders and handlebars. Contrary to what I'd read, the bicycle and pedestrian traffic along the road into and out of Kyambura didn't seem impaired in the slightest.

Still, when Nelson and I stopped and asked a local shopkeeper about the recent attacks, he immediately nodded and pointed to a stretch of maize and millet fields just up the road from us, along the edges of the surrounding Maramagambo Forest. He confirmed that a group of elephants had charged out of the forest one morning two years ago, trampled the fields and nearby gardens, knocked down some huts, and then left. He then pointed to a long red gash in the earth between the planted fields and the forest: a fifteen-foot-deep, twenty-five-foot-wide trench that had been dug by the Uganda Wildlife Authority around the perimeter of Kyambura to keep the elephants at bay and help restore commerce in the vicinity. On the way out of town, Nelson and I would stop to take a closer look at the trench. It was filled with stacks of thorny shrubs for good measure.

"The people are still worried," the shopkeeper told us, shaking his head. "The elephants are just becoming more destructive. I don't know why."

We'd hear similar statements from a number of people in the area, stopping the following day at Kazinga, a fishing village named for the twenty-mile-long channel it overlooks at the heart of Queen Elizabeth, connecting the waters of Lake Edwards with those of Lake George to the north. We parked by the village's small cluster of adobe huts and then walked down a wide, grassy hillside that gently sloped toward the channel's shores.

Groups of fishermen in preposterously tipsy dugout boats were dropping their nets just offshore amid a heaving archipelago of hippo backs, and suddenly I understood the statistic Nelson had mentioned to me about hippos being responsible for by far the highest number of deadly encounters with humans in Africa, most often as a result of fishermen's boats getting too close to nursing mothers. Hippos, their docile, roly-poly appearance notwithstanding, have immensely powerful jaws and swiftly lethal bites.

Still, the people of Kazinga, as those in all the other villages we stopped at that day along the channel, now keep their eyes cast warily landward as well. Only two days prior to my arrival, one fisherman told us, a woman from Kazinga was killed by an elephant. He pointed up the hillside toward an area of forest on the far side of the channel road where he said the woman was attacked while collecting firewood. Two months before that, he told us, outside the village of Katwe at the northern edge of Queen Elizabeth, a man was fatally gored by a young male elephant.

As with chimpanzees and hippos, we've cultivated a mostly benign view of elephants. Floppy-eared dirigibles with six-foot-long probosces do not, after all, readily fit our conception of perfect animal killing machines. Still, elephants are remarkably swift and agile, capable of wielding their tusks with the ceremonious flash and precision of gladiators, often pinning down a victim with one knee to deliver the decisive thrust. Nelson told me a young male Indian tourist had been killed in this fashion two years earlier in Murchison Falls National Park, a few hours north of Queen Elizabeth. He'd made the mistake, Nelson explained, of getting out of his safari vehicle and wandering away from his tour group alone.

It wasn't until near dusk that second day on the road back to the lodge, set high on a bluff above the mouth of Lake Edwards, that the by then mythic specter of the elephant would finally assume solid shape before Nelson and me. We were no more than ten miles from the lodge, driving on a narrow dirt trail on the far shore of Kazinga Channel, when Nelson hit the brakes once again and then pointed at what appeared to be a lone bull elephant grazing among great clumps of acacia and candelabra cactus off to our left.

Nelson figured him to be a rogue—a young male elephant

that usually has made an overly ambitious power play against the dominant male of his herd and been banished, sometimes permanently. Our "rogue," however, soon proved to be one of a massive herd.

All around us, ground vibrations began to register just ahead of the emergence of a cast of at least forty elephants from the nearby trees and brush. We just sat there watching them cross the road, seeming, for all their heft, so light on their feet, soundlessly plying the windswept savanna grasses like land whales adrift above an ancient, waterless sea.

We waited for the entire herd to pass, then had started forward again when from behind a thicket of acacia directly off to our left front bumper a huge female emerged.

"The matriarch," Nelson said softly.

We then noticed the small calf knocking about beneath her, just starting to rip away at a low cluster of acacia branches, the elephants' favorite food. The matriarch held her ground, standing guard, her eyes fixed on us while the calf ate, her back flank blocking most of the road while the rest of the herd milled about in the brush off to our right, a short distance away.

Any elephant herd, I would come to learn, is, in essence, one incomprehensibly massive elephant, a somewhat loosely bound and yet intricately interconnected organism. Calves such as the one Nelson and I were looking at have been shown to stay within fifteen feet of their mothers for nearly all of their first eight years of life. Young elephants are raised within an extended, multitiered network of doting female caregivers that includes the birth mother, grandmothers, aunts, and numerous friends, relations that are maintained over a life span as long as seventy years.

If any harm comes to a member of an elephant group, all the other elephants are aware of it, a sense of cohesion further enforced by an elaborate communication system. In close proximity elephants employ a range of vocalizations, from low-frequency rumbles to higher-pitched screams and trumpets, along with a variety of visual signals, from the waving of their trunks to subtle anglings of the head, body, feet, and tail.

When communicating over long distances—to pass along news about imminent threats, a sudden change of plans, or, of the utmost importance to elephants, the death of a community member—they use patterns of subsonic vibrations that are felt as far as several miles away by exquisitely tuned sensors in the padding of their feet.

Elephants take deaths particularly hard, carefully covering the body of a herd member with earth and brush, conducting weeklong vigils over the deceased, and then making constant revisits over the years to their burial grounds, lifting and caressing the exposed bones with their trunks, taking turns rubbing their trunks along the teeth of a skull's lower jaw the way living elephants do to each other in greeting.

After about fifteen minutes or so, Nelson started inching the Land Rover forward, revving the engine, trying to make us sound as beastly as possible. The matriarch, however, was having none of it, holding her ground, the fierce white of her eyes flaring against the gathering darkness. Although I pretty much knew the answer given the current state of relations between us and elephants, I asked Nelson if he was even considering trying to drive around.

"No," he said, raising an index finger for emphasis. "She'll charge. We're not going anywhere."

I sat perfectly still, staring into that matriarch's white-mad eyes. Into the immense power and woundable intelligence amassed there, and behind the eyes of the others in the herd huddled so close by—a veritable minefield, it now occurred to me, thinking of all I'd been hearing of late about elephant behavior, of pachyderm time bombs.

Just prior to arriving in Uganda, I'd stopped in London to meet with a woman named Eve Abe, a Uganda-born animal ethologist and wildlife management consultant who spent much of her life studying elephants in Queen Elizabeth National Park. In the course of writing her doctorate at Cambridge University about elephants, Abe had a stunning epiphany about the multilayered and intimately related madness behind the breakdown of both elephant and human cultures.

Abe began her studies in Queen Elizabeth back in 1982, as an undergraduate at Makerere University in Kampala, shortly after she and her family, members of the Acholi tribe who'd been living for years as refugees in Kenya to escape the brutal violence in Uganda under the dictatorship of Idi Amin, returned home to northern Uganda in the wake of Amin's ouster in 1979.

When Abe first got to Queen Elizabeth, she said, there were fewer than 150 elephants remaining from an original population of more than 4,000. The bulk of the decimation occurred during Uganda's war with neighboring Tanzania, which led to Amin's overthrow, soldiers from both armies grabbing as much ivory as they could get their hands on with a cravenness that renders the word "poaching" woefully inadequate.

"Normally when you say poaching, you think of people shooting one or two and going off," Abe told me. "But this was war. They'd just throw hand grenades at the elephants, bring whole families down, and then go and cut out the ivory. I call that mass destruction."

Queen Elizabeth's last elephant survivors never left one another's side. They kept in a tight bunch, moving as one. Only one elderly female remained; Abe estimated her to be at least sixty-two. In her soon-to-be-completed memoir *My Elephants, My People,* Abe, who writes of the equal prominence of the matriarch in Acholi society, names that one elephant savior Lady Irene, after her own mother. It was this matriarch, she said, who first gathered the survivors together from their various hideouts on the park's forested fringes and then led them back out as one group into open savanna.

Until her death in the early 1990s, Lady Irene held the group together, the population all the while slowly beginning to rebound. It would take five or six years, Abe said, before she started seeing whole new elephant family units emerge in Queen Elizabeth and begin to split off and go their own way.

By then, Abe's own family was forced to flee the country again. Violence against Uganda's people and elephants never completely abated after Amin's regime collapsed, and it drastically worsened in the course of the full-fledged war that soon developed between government forces and the rebel Lord's Resistance Army.

For years that army's leader, Joseph Kony, routinely "recruited" from Acholi villages in the north, killing the parents of young males before their eyes, often having them do the killings themselves before pressing them into service as child soldiers: kids who eventually returned home to equally ravaged villages, without parents, or schools, or extant societal infrastructure. The majority of the Acholi people now live in one of two hundred displaced-people's camps dispersed throughout northern Uganda.

In the Land Rover that evening, I asked Nelson, also an Acholi, if he'd lost family members in this way. He nodded, said that an uncle of his had been killed, and a few cousins, and a number of family friends. He also said that he knows a number of former *kadogos,* the Ugandan word for child soldiers.

"They have hollow eyes," he told me, his own going blank a moment. "They think nothing of killing. They know no sympathy."

The Lord's Resistance Army has by now been largely defeated, but Kony, who is wanted by the International Criminal Court at The Hague for numerous crimes against humanity, has hidden with what remains of his army in the mountains of Murchison Falls National Park in northwestern Uganda, and more recently in Garamba National Park in the neighboring Democratic Republic of the Congo, where poaching by the Lord's Resistance Army and ongoing wars between rebel factions in the Congo have continued to orphan more elephants.

Many of these orphans, Abe soon realized, have long been part of the yearly elephant migration across the border into Queen Elizabeth National Park, and all at once a picture of parallel cultural breakdowns, human and elephant, began to coalesce in her mind.

"I started looking again at what has happened among the Acholi and the elephants," Abe told me. "I saw that it is an absolute coincidence between the two. Everybody from my tribe lives now within these refugee camps, and there are no more elders. They were systematically eliminated. We are among the lucky few, because my mom and dad managed to escape. But the families there are just broken. I know many of them. Displaced people are living in our former home right now. My mother said let them have it. All these kids who have grown up with their parents killed—no fathers, no mothers, only other children looking after them, and nothing for them to do. No schools. No adult supervision. They form these roaming, violent destructive bands. And it's the same thing that happens with the elephants. They are wild and destructive and completely lost."

Abe has not been back to Uganda since fleeing the country with her mother and a number of her siblings in the late 1980s. She told me that the parallel between the plight of Ugandans and their elephants had in many ways been too close for her to see when she was still living there, that it didn't become apparent to her until she moved to London and had gotten some distance from her past.

I remember asking her at one point why no one else studying elephants had ever made such a connection. She said she had wondered about that herself.

"To me," she said, a tall, elegant woman with a trilling, nearly girlish voice, "it's something I see so clearly now. Most people are scared of showing that kind of anthropomorphism. But coming from me it doesn't sound like I'm inventing something. It's there. People know it's there. Some might think that the way I describe the elephant attacks makes the animals sound like people. But people are animals."

Nelson tried revving the Land Rover's engine again, rocking the vehicle backward and forward, raising clouds of tire-spun dust. The matriarch looked down at us, unimpressed.

She held us there in our tracks for at least another half hour, and even then Nelson gave her and her calf and the rest of their vigilant herd ample time to go on their way before we ventured the last stretch of the Kazinga Channel road.

Back at the lodge that evening—images of that matriarch, and of Eve Abe's wilding bands of orphans, both elephant and human, still playing in my mind like some impossibly far-fetched Hollywood sci-fi script—I sat out on the veranda for a time before going to have dinner, reading over the various elephant studies that the psychologist Gay Bradshaw, who first introduced me to Abe, had authored. Studies in which Bradshaw and a team of researchers, including not only elephant scientists but also experts on such subjects as the effects of trauma on the human brain, essentially set out to codify the sort of intuitive associations that Abe had made about the plight of Uganda's elephants, to see if they also might apply to elephants everywhere.

What they eventually arrived at is nothing less than a portrait of pervasive pachyderm dysfunction, and one that could easily be mistaken for a classic study on human societal breakdown: perhaps the first-ever documented instance of another species' whole-scale psychological and cultural collapse as a result of our own destructive and often dysfunctional behaviors.

One study after the next is filled with the sorts of observations and conclusions I could readily imagine being wielded by a modern-day animal-trial lawyer in the mold of that inspired sixteenth-century defender of rats Bartholomew Chassenee.

I pictured him in the courtroom, pacing back and forth before some slow-blinking, floppy-eared elephant defendant, detailing for judge and jury how decades of habitat loss and poaching, along with systematic culling and translocation of herds by government agencies to control elephant numbers, have completely frayed the fabric of elephant society, disrupting the web of familial and societal relations by which young elephants are raised and established herds are governed.

In herds across the elephants' natural range, Bradshaw and her team found that the number of older matriarchs and female caregivers has drastically fallen, as has the number of elder bulls, who play a significant role in keeping younger males in line. In parts of Africa, a number of the herds studied had no adult females whatsoever. In Uganda, herds were often found to be not the traditional cohesive groups but "semipermanent aggregations," with many females between ages fifteen and twenty-five having no familial associations.

As a result, calves are now being born to and raised by ever younger and inexperienced mothers, and the elephants of these decimated herds, especially the orphans who've witnessed the death of their parents from poaching and culling, are now exhibiting behaviors typically associated with post-traumatic stress disorder and other trauma-related disorders in humans: abnormal startle response, unpredictable asocial behavior, inattentive mothering, and hyperaggression.

Studies done of the raping and slaughtering of the rhinos in South Africa, meanwhile, have shown that in all cases the perpetrators were adolescent males that had witnessed their families being shot down in cullings; orphans for whom it was common to have been tethered to the bodies of their dead and dying relatives until they could be rounded up and transported to locales that often lacked the traditional social hierarchy and cohesive family structures.

Even the few positive developments I read about on the elephant front only lent further substance to the collective elephant-breakdown theory. When South African park rangers recently introduced a number of older bull elephants into several destabilized herds in Pilansberg and Addo national parks, where the raping and killing of rhinos had occurred, the wayward behavior—including the unusually premature hormonal changes among the adolescent elephants—entirely abated.

On and on it went. And just when I imagine Chassenee's courtroom counterpart, the world's greatest animal prosecutor, whoever that might be, standing up and strenuously objecting to the wholly circumstantial and inherently speculative nature of his esteemed colleague's evidence, his "shameless anthropomorphism!" Chassenee pulls out the big guns.

He weighs in with the latest, cutting-edge research in the realm of neuroscience, or what might be called the new physiology of psychology, by which scientists can now map the marred neuronal fields, snapped synaptic bridges, and crooked chemical streams of an embattled psyche. Can isolate highly evolved, specialized neurons such as spindle cells, not only in our brain, but also in the elephant's and the chimp's and those of countless other creatures, and see how severe trauma and stress can render these very florets of the evolving emotional self a bunch of withered and stunted stems.

The first-ever functional MRI scan of an elephant brain, done shortly before I left for Uganda, revealed, perhaps not surprisingly, a huge hippocampus, the seat of memory in all mammalian brains, as well as the same prominent structures in the "limbic system" wherein our brains process emotions; the site of, among other things, spindle cells.

Numerous studies of humans over the past fifty or so years have shown that the development of this emotion-processing region of the brain—the very warp and weave, in other words, of those specialized neurons such as spindle cells and the capacities they help confer: our sense of self-awareness, our ability to both express and regulate emotion, our feelings of empathy—is largely shaped by our life's earliest, prelinguistic experiences, right down to the moment-by-moment exchange of looks between a mother and her infant: the way the mother's gaze repeatedly meets and answers the upward, asking one of the child.

"We know these same brain mechanisms cut across species," Dr. Allan Schore, one of Gay Bradshaw's coauthors and an expert on human trauma, told me on the phone in the days leading up to my trip to Uganda. "In the first years of humans as well as animals like chimps and elephants, the development of the emotional brain is directly affected by what we call attachment mechanisms, by the interactions that an infant has with the primary caregiver, especially the mother. When these early experiences go in positive ways, it leads to greater resilience in things like stress regulation, social communication, and the ability to empathize. But when these early experiences go awry in cases of violence and abuse and neglect, there is a literal thinning down of the essential neuronal circuits in the brain, especially in the emotion-processing areas."

I sat there on the lodge veranda, thinking about this whole other kind of wilderness safari we're now engaged in, where we're now aware of the number of frayed neuronal circuits in the brains of our fellow creatures.

If not so long ago we humans were still balking at the idea that one of our own species, a soldier, for example, could be physically wounded by psychological harm—the idea, in other words, that the mind is not an entity apart from the body and therefore just as woundable as any limb—we now find ourselves having to make an equally profound and, for many, even more difficult leap: that creatures such as Roger, or Ripley, or Mary the elephant are as precisely and intricately woundable as we are; that sudden, violent outbursts such as Mary's or Topsy's, or Ollie's and Buddy's out at Animal Haven Ranch; or the tortured dreams, and white haired demons, and asocial days of retirees like Roger here, can not only no longer be dismissed as anecdotal, arbitrary events, the isolated revolts of a strange, rare few against the inevitable constraints and abuses of captivity. They also may be harbingers of the sorts of behavior we can now expect from the remaining few in the wild.

Far across Kazinga Channel that evening, I could see the shoreward glistening hippos and Nile crocodiles, the nearby grazing herds of water buffalo, and, farther up the hillside, the drifting groups of elephants, alternately plying and pulling at their lush pods of acacia. It all looked to me like some distant, passing reenactment of wilderness, a dream version of the wild that we had to conquer the actual place in order to stage.

They have no future without us, the chimps, elephants, whales, and the rest. None. The question that we, the keepers, are facing is whether we'd mind a future without them, among the more mindful creatures on Earth and, in many ways, the more devoted; whether we'd be bothered by an Earth with no living vestiges of our own differently shaped selves.

I remember as Nelson and I were waiting to pass along the Kazinga Channel road earlier that evening, he told me something peculiar about the incident two months before in which the man from the nearby village of Katwe had been killed by a young male elephant.

He said the elephant's herd came back and buried the deceased as they would one of their own, carefully covering the body with earth and brush and then standing vigil over it. When a group of villagers went to reclaim the man's body for his own family's funeral rites, the elephants refused to budge. Human remains, a number of researchers have observed, are the only other ones that elephants will treat as devoutly as they do their own.

Highly social animals, it only follows, feel more deeply death's rip at the social fabric. Chimps and other fellow primates, whales and dolphins, even a number of bird species, have all been observed exhibiting what is known as "separation distress" over the loss of mates, parents, or offspring. Chimp and gorilla mothers will carry a dead infant around with them for days before letting the decaying corpse go. Adult chimps have been known to pine away to the point of starvation over the loss of a close companion.

It dawned on me as Nelson was talking about that elephant herd in Katwe how so many of the very animal cultures we're

destroying prefigured our own, the first permanent human set–
tlements having sprung up around the desire of our earliest
nomadic tribal ancestors to stay by the graves of their dead.
"The city of the dead," as historian and philosopher Lewis
Mumford wrote, "antedates the city of the living; necropolis
prefigured metropolis."

In the end, Nelson said, the people of Katwe were forced to
resort to a tactic deeply etched by now in the elephants' collective memory: firing volleys of gunfire into the air at close range
to finally scare the mourning herd away.

Roger has finally stopped.

Four fifty A.M. He's just sitting there in the middle of his room, amid the magazines and Yellow Pages, both hands lying limp on either side of him, palms up, eyes staring blankly off. He looks exhausted.

Outside the areaway doors, night, like a newly restarted wind-up toy, whirs on in soft, intermeshing gears: crickets, peepers, the occasional owl, and just seconds ago, one far-off, droning Cessna, flying wherever at this hour.

I can't help wondering now if this air-piling of Roger's might not have been a reenactment of something he remembers doing with the person that he thinks I am.

That, of course—like just about everything else between Roger and me this week—is the sort of conjecture I could have dismissed long ago if he and his ilk weren't so bright and their memories so damn precise.

Just the other day I read in the newspaper about an adult male orangutan named Sibu. He was recently recruited by the caretakers of a primate park in Amsterdam to be their breeding male, but has thus far shown interest only in human females, and of a very particular type: tall blondes with lots of tattoos, the very description, it turns out, of his first keeper.

Chimps, too, form these early and lasting bonds with us. I witnessed the very thing in the course of the next stop in my travels after Chimp Party, an experience that has been haunting me ever since Roger sounded those hand claps a week ago.

I did end up driving into St. Louis upon leaving Mike Casey's house that night and decided to get myself a hotel room directly across from the famed Gateway Arch, having never seen the thing in person. I ate a late dinner and then sat up in my room for some time, staring at the arch and the adjacent, light-flecked waters of the Mississippi River, thinking all the while about this endgame moment we're coming to now with so many of the Earth's animals and wondering what form, if any, their sanctuary might finally take.

The following morning I decided that rather than starting back home I would head farther south, to Shreveport, Louisiana, to look at Chimp Haven, the new, federally funded retirement home for former research lab chimpanzees that was just then in its final stages of construction.

There are still some twelve hundred chimpanzees in the United States used in research, most of them for various medical and pharmaceutical protocols (everything from injecting them with hepatitis and malaria in hopes of developing vaccines to drug toxicity testing to determine the proper dosage levels for us), and the rest for language and intelligence studies.

Nearly a thousand more chimps, however, have long been out of service, the unintended "surplus" of a frenzied captive-chimpanzee breeding program that the government began back in the 1980s in the mistaken expectation that chimps would be a perfect lab model for the development of a vaccine against HIV—a disease we've since discovered chimps rarely contract, most likely because it originated as a simian virus that then made what is known as a "zoonotic leap" to humans. Of these surplus chimps, more than three hundred have already been slated for retirement to Chimp Haven.

I got a bit lost trying to find the place and somehow wound up instead at the entrance to the nearby Forcht-Wade Correctional Center. I pulled up to the gatehouse. Nobody there knew anything about Chimp Haven.

"We got a new retirement facility here for aging lifers," one of the guards announced proudly, pointing to a white, concrete monolith with narrow barred windows on the far side of the front fence.

The other guard made a call on the gatehouse phone. He then came out, told me to park my car and wait. Moments later a prison van arrived. The front gate slid open. I was directed to get inside the van. The driver took me all of a hundred yards, past a lone picnic table set inside a small cement yard bound in bright, sun-bitten swirls of concertina wire, then dropped me off at the prison's administration building.

Inside, I signed in at the front desk and was soon met there by an assistant warden named Anthony D. Batson. When I explained to Warden Batson that I was looking for Chimp Haven, his eyes brightened.

"Took a tour of the place just last week," he said. "Tell you what: theirs is a modern, first-class facility. Got rooms bigger than ours. We could probably take a couple of tips from them."

Upon getting the proper directions, I asked the warden if the inmates knew about their new neighbors. He told me they were certainly aware of Chimp Haven, having access to TV and newspapers, and doing occasional work in the area, but that he hadn't heard them express any opinions about it.

"A number of guys have asked me what would happen if one of the chimps gets out," he said. "Whether they'd have to go get it. But we both have our own escape procedures. They're on top of it over there. Of course, they tranquilize. We don't tranquilize."

Chimp Haven was only days away from receiving its first retirees, and everywhere people were scurrying about to prepare the place. In the facility's indoor housing units, workers were doing final sweeps of the chimps' spacious sleeping quarters, complete with fresh running water and cross-ventilation, multiple windows and skylights, hammocks made of neatly cross-hatched sections of used fire hose, bedding of warm blankets and hay, and vanity mirrors. And, of course, wall sockets for ready access to the facility's plastic-covered home-entertainment equipment.

Through an elaborate system of sliding doors and overhead walkways, all the rooms led either to the indoor medical and dental clinics, or outside to private patios and playgrounds and, just beyond those, walled and moated five-acre expanses of vine-laced pine and sweet-gum forest.

Touring Chimp Haven's huge main kitchen, I saw refrigerator shelves lined with rows of "apesicles"—plastic cups filled with frozen-juice suspensions of raw vegetables and fruit. Against the opposite wall, alongside a popcorn maker, stood a massive container of primate biscuits—essentially dry hunks of vitamin-and protein-enriched kibble.

Set out on a long metal food-preparation table were rows of turf boards: square sections of thick plastic covered with Astro-Turf onto which staff workers were getting ready to smear a mixture of peanut butter, nuts, and seeds, which the chimps must ferret out with their fingers. Insofar as the better part of a chimpanzee's day in the wild is spent foraging for food, many of the enrichment devices they're given are geared toward alleviating the boredom of having three squares regularly served up to them.

A full, healthy sex life among the chimps also is encouraged, but not before all the males receive vasectomies. The last thing places such as Chimp Haven or the Center for Great Apes want is more chimps. Aside from the unnatural constraints of captivity on a wild animal, each one costs about $20,000 a year to house and maintain.

All aspects of life at Chimp Haven have been carefully considered in this way, everything from physical and psychological therapists for the retirees to help them overcome the past stresses and traumas of life as research lab subjects to grief counselors when one of the chimps passes away. Even the walled-off wedges of forest have been arranged so the chimps there also can see back to the familiar hustle and bustle of the facility's main human complex.

These are animals who, like Roger and the others here at the Center for Great Apes, have been so "encultured" by us that to now fully deprive them of human contact would constitute the next form of abuse. Thus Chimp Haven: a veritable chimpanzee Jurassic Park, a shining example of just how far we can extend the paradox of trying to liberate and dignify a wild creature within captivity.

In the old inner city zoo ape houses of my youth, all the inhabitants got was the equivalent of a tiled public lavatory stall with a token section of chained log inside and a metal nameplate secured out front, a dot on a silhouette of Africa indicating the captive's original home. By the exit of those old ape houses there was typically one of those silly fun-house mirrors with bars painted in front and a caption that read, "The Most Dangerous Ape of Them All." Chimp Haven struck me as being the result of a long, serious look in that mirror. A possible reflection of our wild counterparts' only future sanctuary: the prototype for a new kind of humanzee city in which we'll be preserving the last remnants of our primal ancestry, a world of highly enculturated, Roger-like "cosmo-chimps," forever suspended on man-made jungle gyms and makeshift tree vines somewhere between their true selves and us. Chimps that we might even breed over time, as dogs have been, for just the right personality traits and temperaments, and for all manner of work, from the strictly utilitarian—fighting our wars and working in our factories—to the increasingly abstract: our own personalized pet primitives, living, sweet-musk keepsakes of what we humans have been trying to both renounce and remember in ourselves all along.

After getting my tour that day, I was invited back to Chimp Haven's downtown Shreveport headquarters to meet the facility's executive director, Linda Koebner. A lifetime New Yorker like myself, Koebner is something of a pioneer in chimp retirement. Back in 1974, she transferred nine chimpanzees from a no-longer-operational primate research facility in upstate New York to a new home on their own island in a habitat facility known as Lion Country Safari, in Loxahatchee, Florida.

Koebner escorted me into a back conference room at one point to show me some film clips of the chimps' initial arrival on that island. It was some time before three of the chimps—Swing, Spark, and Doll—could even be coaxed out of their cages once they'd been set down on the island, having known only confinement until then.

Doll, when she finally emerged, shot up to the top of the nearest tree. Spark clutched his cage even as he was leaving it, and then nestled alongside the open door, where he ripped away an attached packing slip and put it over his face. He kept gingerly pawing at the ground with his hand, as though to test this new surface's reliability.

Koebner, for her own safety, had to observe all this from the far side of the island's moat. But a full nineteen years later she returned to Lion Country Safari and, accompanied by a habitat employee wielding a movie camera, was allowed to try a first-hand visit with the chimps she had freed.

In the film, you can see a couple of the chimps beginning to come slowly forward from the far side of the island as Koebner's boat makes its way across the moat, and then the chimps are quickly striding toward the same climbing platform that the boat is fast approaching.

"Hey . . . remember me?" Koebner keeps repeating in a soft, breathy voice to Swing and Doll, the two of them waiting now at the very edge of the climbing platform.

As the boat arrives, Koebner pauses a moment, then stands and reaches up across the prow. Within seconds, she is being enveloped, her slight frame slipping in and out of deep, alternating hugs from Swing and Doll, each politely waiting their turn for another embrace of their now sobbing liberator.

Four fifty-four A.M. Roger is walking bolt upright in my direction. Seeing him like this, striding forward in this manner, only underscores at once how human he is and yet how much more grand and powerful.

He could kill me so easily that it somehow only heightens my desire to let him. To find some way inside his room and just have him end our mutual journeying in that manner, there being no other means, in the end, of us getting where we each want to go, no way of escaping our respective cages.

I've been, as I say, over and over it. Have thought back countless times, trying to come up with some instance in my past, however fleeting, in which Roger and I could have possibly crossed paths.

There have been, as far as I know, only three chimp encounters in my life in the years since Roger's birth. They all, strangely enough, took place that same summer of 1979 when Roger would have been less than a year old; and like the last of those three encounters—that bizarre Airstream visitation on Manhattan's Lower East Side—the other two happened nowhere near Roger's longtime home state of Florida.

The first occurred in the old ape house at the Central Park Zoo in Manhattan. I got into an intense stare-down there one summer afternoon with a young male chimp. They are always the most willing to engage. The exchange easily outlasted two or three waves of visitors. When we were finally alone, the chimp picked up a bag of peanuts someone had tossed toward the front of his enclosure and held it toward me. I looked around to make sure no one was watching, reached forward to take it, and the chimp yanked it away at the last second, breaking into delighted fits of hoots and pants.

Weeks later, I was out on the opposite coast visiting a friend in Portland, Oregon. We went to the zoo one afternoon. I, as usual, got caught up in the ape house, locked eyes there with another young male chimp. He, just like his East Coast counterpart, waited until we were all alone, then stood and made his way to the far back of his enclosure: the classic white-tiled, subway bathroom with the chained log inside and an actual washroom sink set against the back wall.

I watched the chimp briefly bend over the sink, then turn and make his way back. He politely took his place before me again and resumed our stare-down, holding a stolid expression for at least another few minutes before fully dousing my face with a mouthful of water.

I took both of these episodes, even then, as early confirmations of that aptitude (I'm not sure if that's the word), that natural disposition of mine—and it's one that I believe Roger recognized in me straightaway—to outwait those irritable, alien entanglements and antsy tugs of the human brain's added spindle cells. To abide such long stretches of pure thoughtlessness that I am soon being lured by the sound of that same inner bog voice into the mental lacunae, the primordial lagoons, of our brain's earlier evolved states, regions where one encounters preincarnated, deeply inculcated animal selves far less familiar than the likes of Roger here.

I would meet some of those other selves in the midst of my recent explorations of the new science of "animal personality." I remember one night in particular when I was allowed to roam alone after closing hours through the darkened corridors of the Seattle Aquarium for a prearranged interlude with a giant Pacific octopus (GPO) there named Achilles.

It is an eerie, spectral place, a big-city aquarium at night. With the lights turned down in the empty viewing galleries, the luminous fish dioramas fairly swell against your senses, rendering *you* now the viewed and startled captive, adrift in your own natural medium, in a literal suspension of disbelief.

I went from one walled and lighted day to the next, the multicolored fish adrift among their submerged tree and coral branches like birds in some flip side of the sky. Slowly making my way toward the center of the aquarium's main viewing gallery, I then arrived at the huge, twelve-foot-high glass tank of Achilles.

There are, as fellow life-forms go, few as deeply alien— in both substance and appearance—as the giant Pacific octopus. Adults can weigh more than a hundred pounds, and yet all of their throbbing, multitentacled mass can pass like water through a drain pipe no bigger in circumference than an apple, just wide enough to accommodate the octopus's cartilaginous beak, its only solid body part. They look, at rest, like cracked leather discards from a handbag factory; in motion, like windswept hot-air balloons in severe deflation distress, with no one at home in the balloon's gondola but a pair of unsettlingly knowing black eyes.

It was those eyes more than anything that I had asked the aquarium's director, Roland Anderson, for special permission to stare into on my own. Just me and Achilles alone—excellent training, now that I think of it, for the far shorter journey I've been making here with Roger—with no other aquarium visitors around to make me self-conscious about doing things such as tapping my fingers on the glass in hopes of getting Achilles riled, or reading impossible complexities into his muffled side of the conversation. For behaving, in short, in a way that even I— the deeply contented resident of a retirement home for former ape actors—would have considered preposterous had I not heard Anderson's real-life octopus stories earlier that day.

Anderson told me that he and his staff first started naming the GPOs at the Seattle Aquarium twenty years ago. Not out of cutesy sentimentality. Anderson, a longtime marine biologist and the son of a sea captain, made it clear that he is not given to that sort of thing. It was, he said, because they couldn't help noticing the animals' distinct personalities.

GPOs live about three or four years, and the aquarium typically keeps three on the premises—two on display and one backup or understudy octopus—so there have been a good number of them at the aquarium over the past two decades. Still, Anderson had little trouble recalling them: Emily Dickinson, for example, a particularly shy, retiring female GPO who always hid behind the tank's rock outcroppings, or Leisure Suit Larry, who, Anderson told me, would have been arrested in our world for sexual assault, with his arms always crawling all over passing researchers. And then there was Lucretia McEvil. She repeatedly tore her tank apart at night, scraping away all the rocks at the base, pulling up the water filter, biting through nylon cables, all the parts left floating on the surface when Anderson arrived in the morning.

One particularly temperamental GPO so disliked having his tank cleaned that he would keep grabbing the cleaning tools, trying to pull them and the cleaner into the tank with him, his skin going a bright red, something octopuses do when they get extremely riled. Another took to regularly soaking one of the aquarium's female night biologists with the water funnel octopuses normally use to propel themselves, because he didn't like it when she shined her flashlight into his tank.

Anderson has known the extremely aggressive octopus, the more laid-back, let-the-food-come-to-me kind, and the preternaturally shy type, those who are content to rummage alone through scraps later, after all the others have cleared away, and then will leave their own discards in neat piles for the attendants to find the next morning.

He has dealt with the provincial, stay-at-home octopuses and the irrepressible wanderers with Houdini-like escape skills rivaling those of our next of kin. Anderson arrived one morning to find an octopus clear across the other side of the main viewing gallery, dining on some of the crabs and starfish in the aquarium's Northern Pacific coastline diorama. Another morning he found a GPO a good ways up the ramp leading toward the aquarium's rear exit door.

Just across from Achilles that night was another GPO, a female named Mikala, their two tanks connected by an overhead, see-through passageway. The passageway's doors were closed for now, but in the coming months the aquarium's scientists would be opening them in hopes of mating Mikala with Achilles.

At one point I decided to absent myself from Achilles' probing stare and walk around beneath the overhead passageway between the two tanks to see if I could look at Mikala in hers. I found her sound asleep, mushed between the tank's outer glass and some craggy rocks. I considered tapping the glass to see if I could stir her, but decided that was a bit rude and let her be. When I turned around, Achilles was bobbing right there behind me, two black eyes bulging now against the backdrop of his bright red skin.

"How do we even define what an emotion is in an animal?" Anderson had asked earlier. "And why do they even have these different temperaments?"

And they have them, we are now finding, all up and down and across life's branches: adumbrations of our very selves, our individual identities, found in every creature we can look at.

In the weeks following my visit with Achilles and Mikala, I would meet with a number of different scientists who, like superannuated daydreaming children with their noses pressed to simulated pond shores, and glass-framed ant farms and fish tanks, are staring at everything from frogs and lizards and spiders to stickleback fish, pond striders, and fruit flies, documenting in one species after the next the same palette of behavioral traits we all recognize in one another: the reckless daredevil versus the cautious, risk-averse type; the aggressive bully and his or her meek victims; the sensitive, reactive individuals versus those not cursed with an overabundance of self-awareness—straight-ahead, proactive types wholly oblivious to how their behaviors are affecting others.

One biology professor I met at the University of California at Davis named Judy Stamps was studying how early life experiences affect habitat selection in drosophila, better known as the common fruit fly. Stamps escorted me one afternoon to a Biology Department "animal room," where she and her students had been conducting their experiments.

The room was no bigger than a small walk-in closet, barely large enough to contain the eleven-foot-long metal table before us. For the fruit fly, however, this was the site of epic interplanetary journeys and pitched struggles for survival. Set at either end of the table were bizarrely shaped, artificial fruit-bowl habitats made of upward-twisting wire designed to hold, like a Victorian orrery, different fruit planets: plums, apples, pears, and so on. Ones that, Stamps has discovered, fruit flies will approach and attempt to settle on in a number of different ways depending on their early life experiences and their different personalities.

Fruit flies born and raised on a plum, for example, will always seek out the next plum to settle on, as will their offspring: a "no place like home" impulse in fruit flies. Stamps and her students also have encountered everything from overly shy, timorous fruit fly pilgrims, to bold trailblazers, to downright feisty, pugnacious, and ultimately self-defeating bullies, flies that would spend all day knocking other flies off of a piece of fruit, declaring themselves the ruler of a given banana or peach, but who, when it came time to mate, would end up all alone.

Why nature would create such a broad palette of behaviors even in creatures with little or no mind to reflect on or argue with the ways they behave is a question scientists are now pondering. The prevailing theory among the different researchers I spoke with suggests that insofar as a particular trait will serve a given species' survival chances in one set of circumstances, and a wholly different trait in another, evolution has crafted all manner of attitudes and temperaments to suit existence's ever-shifting challenges.

There seems to be little question anymore, however, about the somewhat paradoxical fact that personality is not exclusive to people. About the fact that the templates for all forms of emotion and behavior—in all creatures—were shaped by the same evolutionary forces that inspire the beatings of a fly's wings, or that of our own hearts, or the manic rubbing of a disturbed chimpanzee's fingers along his bottom row of teeth.

Four fifty-seven A.M. Roger is right back here at the front bars, but still standing, looming above me. A massive wall of near-man and yet not menacing. Just that warm, familiar scent and a self, a "someone" I still can't quite place, poised for discovery.

Of the strange troika of chimps I encountered that late summer of 1979, the diapered Airstream baby is still the one that I would most like to have been Roger. I suppose because he, like Roger, appeared in the most unlikely way and yet seemed at once and impossibly familiar.

I happened to be on my front stoop that morning because I was waiting for the arrival of a friend in a rented moving truck into which I was about to load my life's belongings and begin a long drive south to Houston, Texas, where I'd recently been offered a teaching job.

I sat there sipping my coffee, watching a construction crew dig a huge hole at the nearby intersection of Third Street and Second Avenue in Manhattan, layer-cake-like sections of former streets and sewer and gas pipes being methodically lifted out and set off to one side, the few pedestrians out at that early hour all stopping, as city dwellers do, to stare into the hole: the sudden gap in the seemingly impregnable argument for ourselves that is a city.

I felt at one point a large, rumbling shadow encroach from over my left shoulder and turned to see not the moving truck but a shiny new Airstream RV pulling up to the curb alongside me. It idled there a moment and then the engine shut off, the side door opened, and out onto the sidewalk stepped the diapered would-be Roger.

The memory of that chimp came back to me so clearly just the other afternoon as Roger and I were sitting here together watching *Tarzan's New York Adventure*. Roger's interest in the movie, I noticed, spiked whenever Cheeta appeared on-screen. But at that one scene, lasting no more than a few seconds, in which Cheeta hops out of the New York City taxi in advance of Tarzan and Jane and stands there alone on the sidewalk, Roger, just as he had done with that bonobo on the cover of

The Metaphysics of Apes, sat bolt upright and pressed his nose through the bars.

And all at once it was the late summer of '79 again, and I was sitting out on that Lower East Side stoop, looking at this baby chimpanzee, not even a year old, wearing only the pair of diapers inside rubber pants and an expression as startled as mine must have been, the two of us no more than the length of one of his lanky arms from each other.

He stood there, blinking back the morning sunlight, raising his right hand at one point to the prowlike ridge of his brow to shade his view, and then he took in the surrounding buildings and street and, down at the near end of the block, the scene of the digging construction crew. He then craned his head back in my direction and locked eyes with mine.

We kept like that for what seemed a good long time before he slowly began to lift his left hand. To wave at me, I thought at first, then realized that he perhaps wanted me to take hold of it, something I was briefly considering doing when at the other end of a long, thin neck tether that I hadn't noticed until then the young chimp's owner stepped out from the door of the Airstream, laughing heartily over what had clearly become a favorite prank of his.

I can't recall now what this man looked like or if we ever exchanged words. Some people from the neighborhood had already begun to approach by then, and from the other, far end of the block, a small band of Hells Angels were coming up the sidewalk from the group's Third Street headquarters near the intersection of First Avenue.

Among them was one of the Angels' reputed leaders, "Mike the Bike." He and I didn't know one another personally, but it so happened that a few nights earlier, Mike's "sort of ex-girlfriend," as she was later described to me by a local bartender, had exchanged some friendly words with me at the bar—she, in fact, gave me her phone number—and all within full view of Mike.

I sat staring at this baby chimpanzee staring back at me, his hand still suspended, midgesture, in the air; his owner cackling away; the neighbors' voices closing in on my right; Mike the Bike and company approaching from the other direction, coming ever closer. I took a last look at the young chimp and then, in a moment of simultaneously deep longing and dread, I fled.

It wasn't until I was back upstairs, huddled breathlessly against my third-story apartment window, looking down on the stoop below, that I felt certain it was the chimp and not I that Mike the Bike was on his way to see.

Everyone was milling about by then, talking and laughing with the Airstream's owner. But every so often, his diapered pet would venture away from the crowd to the very end of his tether, standing out there alone on the sidewalk, staring quizzically up at the sun-splashed facade of building windows into which I had disappeared.

Four fifty-nine A.M. Roger is seated again, settled back exactly where he was when this night began. He has even eschewed the askance, confessor stance: his huge shoulders square to mine once more; his body gently rocking; the flaring, hazel-eyed stare further enveloping me, inviting me in; that left forefinger wrapped around the central crossbar, poised, as ever, for the taking.

"Go on," the bog voice intones, and I'm watching my hand again now, moving through the air—tendinous, vibratory—beyond the painted red line, even as another voice, clearer and, sadly, more reasoned, keeps reminding me how one touch could either be the very thing that Roger needs, all that he's been waiting for, or all it would take to fully reawaken him to his own worst fears, instantly undoing whatever progress we may have made.

They do recover, the animals, even some of the more severely traumatized among them. It has been seen with a number of the brains in Dr. Hof's cooler: ours, the chimp's, the elephant's. The healing of the traumatized mammal mind turns out to have the same physical correlatives as the wounding does, the brain, through therapies now being applied to humans and animals alike, forging new neurons and neuronal connections outside the stunted and scarred regions.

Shortly after my return from Uganda, I visited a place called the Elephant Sanctuary in Tennessee, a twenty-seven-hundred-acre rehabilitation center and retirement facility in the state's verdant, low-rolling southern hill country. The sanctuary is a kind of asylum for some of the more emotionally and psychologically disturbed former zoo and circus elephants in the United States—cases so bad that the people who profited from them were eager to let them go.

Of the nineteen residents I met at the Elephant Sanctuary, the biggest hard-luck story was one strikingly similar to that of the ill-fated Mary, hung back in 1916 from that railway car in Erwin, Tennessee.

A five-ton Asian elephant like Mary, Misty was originally captured as a calf in India in 1966. She spent her first decade in captivity with a number of American circuses and finally ended up in the early 1980s at a wild-animal attraction known as Lion Country Safari in Irvine, California. It was there, on the afternoon of July 25, 1983, that Misty, one of four performing elephants at Lion Country Safari that summer, somehow managed to break free from her chains and began madly dashing about the park, looking to make an escape. When one of the park's zoologists tried to corner and contain her, Misty killed him with one swipe of her trunk.

Compared with Mary's fate, however, Misty's seems a triumph of modern humanism. Banished, after the Lion Country Safari killing, to the Hawthorn Corporation, a company in Illinois that trains and leases elephants and tigers to circuses, she would continue to lash out at a number of her trainers over the years. But when Hawthorn was convicted of numerous violations of the Animal Welfare Act in 2003, the company agreed to relinquish custody of Misty to the Elephant Sanctuary. She was loaded onto a transport trailer on the morning of November 17, 2004, and even then managed to get away with one final shot at the last in her life's long line of captors.

Carol Buckley, one of the Elephant Sanctuary's founders, told me the afternoon I visited that the owner of Hawthorn was trying to get Misty to stretch out so he could remove her leg chains before loading her on the trailer. At one point he apparently gave Misty a prod behind the ear with a bull hook, the very thing that set Mary off years ago, and she knocked the owner down with a quick swipe of the trunk.

"But we've seen nothing like that since she's been here," Buckley said, the two of us pulling up on her all-terrain four-wheeler to a large, grassy enclosure where an extremely docile and contented-looking Misty, trunk high, ears flapping, waited to greet us. "She's as sweet as can be. You'd never know that this elephant killed anybody."

In the course of her more than two years at the Elephant Sanctuary—much of it spent in quarantine while undergoing daily treatment for tuberculosis—Misty also has been in therapy, as in psychotherapy, to help her overcome the traumas common to orphaned animal captives: being taken from parents whose slaughter they've often witnessed and then dispatched to a foreign environment to work as performers or laborers, all the while being kept in confinement and relative isolation.

Now under the Elephant Sanctuary's system of passive control, one modeled on a number of basic human trauma therapy principles, Misty has been free to come and go in a safe environment, to make all her own choices without any form of coercion, and to live in the company of a larger established community of elephants.

Buckley said Misty seemed to sense straight off the different feeling of her new home. When one of the caretakers went to free Misty's still-chained leg a mere day after she'd arrived, she stood peaceably by, practically offering her leg up. Over her many months of quarantine, meanwhile, with only humans acting as a kind of surrogate elephant family, she has consistently gone through the daily rigors of her tuberculosis treatments—involving two caretakers, a team of veterinarians, and the use of a restraining chute in which harnesses are secured about her chest and tail—without any coaxing or pressure.

"We'll shower her with praise in the barn afterwards," Buckley told me as Misty stood by, chomping on a mouthful of hay, "and she actually purrs with pleasure. The whole barn vibrates."

The Elephant Sanctuary's approach also is being applied to wild elephants in both Africa and India. At one refuge in Kenya known as the David Sheldrick Wildlife Trust, the caregivers essentially serve as surrogate mothers to young orphaned elephants, gradually restoring their psychological and emotional well-being to the point at which they can be reintroduced into existing wild herds.

The human "allomothers" stay by their adopted young orphans' sides, even sleeping with them at night in stables. But the caretakers make sure to rotate from one elephant to the next. Otherwise a young elephant will form such a strong bond with one keeper that if that person is absent for any extended period, the elephant begins to grieve as if over the loss of a family member, often becoming physically ill in the human mother's absence.

So far more than a hundred elephants from the David Sheldrick Wildlife Trust have been successfully reintroduced into wild herds. A number of them have periodically returned to the refuge with their own wild-born calves to have reunions with their human foster parents and introduce their offspring to what is now being recognized—at least by the elephants—as a whole new subspecies; yet another evolutionary anomaly that only we could have created: "the homo-pachyderm allogrand-mother."

Somehow, we've arrived at the point where the only chance for the likes of Roger and a number of the species we're now driving to distraction is for us to learn enough about them and their ways to allow us to better mitigate the ruinous effects of our own. To finally get past ourselves and our story and, through acts of deep, interspecies empathy—or what Gay Bradshaw refers to in her writing as a new "trans-species psyche"—to become a part of their story. Become, in effect, better animals.

Five oh-five A.M. Night is winding down now, that deep quiet before first light's familiar shift of sounds.

The others will be up before very long, the clamor of their hoots and cries filling the morning air, followed by that of the caretakers clanking cage doors and sliding walkway chutes.

And yet here sits Roger, front and center, wide-eyed and eager as ever.

I will go home soon, and soon be going truly home. Will don, however begrudgingly, embarrassedly, the man mantle again: "the most dangerous ape of them all," and by far—as Roger has, in his own nonrebuking way, repeatedly reminded me this past week—the most entrapped.

But what of Roger? What possible mirror effect might the elemental migrations and assuagements he has allowed me have, in turn, on him, so that the simple act of my going off to grab some sleep tonight won't have to be his undoing?

When, I keep wondering—not a whole lot of darkness left now—will Roger's Misty-like moment of deliverance come, his restitution: Roger finally able to sleep at night and mix with the others by day, the whole of the Center for Great Apes vibrating with his cries of happiness?

When he believes that I finally recognize him? And then

what? Will that free Roger to go back toward some semblance of his original self (whatever that even is anymore) or only further propel him in the direction we've been suggesting to him all along: the incurable humanzee; the chimp who either can't or just flat-out refuses to remember how to be one?

As resistant as Roger has been thus far to all rehabilitation efforts, I have seen chimps in my recent travels who, just like us and the elephants, have been able to bounce back from the most extreme abuses.

In her office at Chimp Haven headquarters in downtown Shreveport, Linda Koebner mentioned to me a woman named Carole Noon, who, she said, was currently liberating hundreds of chimpanzees from a notorious former biomedical research facility in Alamogordo, New Mexico, known as the Coulston Foundation, methodically delivering ten chimps at a time in monthly trailerloads to her new multi-island refuge in Fort Pierce, Florida.

Upon leaving Shreveport, I decided to head a bit farther south, to Houston, to visit an old friend, and from there tried to contact Carole Noon. She happened to be in Alamogordo when I finally tracked her down, but was, she told me, on her way back to Florida the day after next, leaving me a narrow one-day window for what Noon referred to as my "tour of hell."

I got a flight to El Paso early the following morning, then rented a car for the three-hour drive north through the blank, hardscrabble high desert of southern New Mexico to Alamogordo, home of Holloman Air Force Base, test pilots and young air force trainees regularly scorching the skies above the roadway as I drove.

The air force base, I later learned, is also home to the Alamagordo Primate Facility, containing 241 chimpanzees leased from the government by a Massachusetts-based pharmaceutical company primarily conducting hepatitis C research. Just beyond Holloman, I passed through the White Sands Missile Range, site of the first atomic bomb tests as well as a variety of ongoing missile and rocket payload launchings. A corner of the world, in short, just empty enough to allow for everything from the concussive splitting of an atom to the screams of hundreds of caged and disease-riddled chimpanzees without so much as a blip on our collective human radar.

Having arrived at the Coulston Foundation—a bleak assemblage of rust-colored corrugated tin buildings on Alamagordo's western fringes—more than an hour early for my meeting with Carole Noon, I decided to pay a quick visit to the International Space Hall of Fame. It's situated on the far side of Alamogordo and, like everything else in its wide-open vicinity, plainly visible from Coulston's front entrance: a giant gold-mirrored cube alongside a tall white rocket ship set hard against the pale red, Martian tint of the Sacramento Mountains.

The place looks like something straight out of a 1950s-era B-list sci-fi film, its front courtyard bedecked with all manner of missiles, space capsules, and rocket-engine parts, some whole and shiny, others crushed, melted, and misshapen, like Dali's drooping clocks. Inside, I got to sit in a Mercury space capsule and to execute a simulated space shuttle landing. Near the museum's exit I came upon a little exhibit devoted to the "chimponauts," the pioneering space-flight chimps who endured everything from decompression-chamber and zero-gravity tests to whirling in high-speed centrifuges, often passing out or having their internal organs explode from the extreme g-forces.

There were, of course, a number of shots of Ham and Enos. In January 1961, the three-year-old Ham became the first non-human primate in outer space. Eleven months later, the five-year-old Enos did a complete orbit of the Earth, maintaining his focus despite a malfunction in his capsule's control panel that gave him an electric shock rather than the intended reward each time he performed the correct maneuver. Enos died in a cage a year later at only six.

It was near dusk when I drove back over to Coulston and met Carole Noon in the facility's former headquarters. She promptly escorted me out a back door toward the main chimp compound. An unseasonably cold wind stirred dust and tumbleweed across Alamogordo's treeless outskirts. Shrill screams and the clamor of pounded cages began to fill the early evening air.

Dinnertime, Noon explained, was the usual catalyst for such a display, but tonight it was my unfamiliar presence that had everyone going. We were still some seventy-five yards from Building 700—the first in a series of eight long, single-story chimp residences that make up Coulston's barrackslike assemblage—when the ruckus began: those slow, hollow, bellyborne whoops quickly swelling into piercing shrieks, followed by intense cage pounding, the same pattern repeating itself from one building to the next, off into the distance.

"How's our boy Ollie doing?" Noon muttered into her walkie-talkie.

A husky-voiced woman in her late forties with piercing blue eyes and long, sandy-blond hair tied back beneath a Save the Chimps cap, Noon was asking after a resident of Building 700 named Oliver, an adolescent male who'd had the cornea of his right eye badly scratched in a tussle with another chimp and needed to be anesthetized to be treated.

"Still sleeping," came the reply.

The better part of Building 700's facade was, like all the others at the facility, covered in thick sheets of plastic to hold in the heat around the chimps' newly expanded outer cages during the winter and early spring. I therefore didn't see the advance scout for the building's fifty-nine other chimps until Noon and I were about to enter: a massive, thick-limbed male hovering directly above us, clutching the uppermost reaches of his cell, trying to size me up through the same murky polymer prism that was rendering him a dark apparition in some drug-induced dream.

"In the old days," Noon explained, "they couldn't even go out in the cold months. Now they can at least be outside when they want, and we get a chance to really clean out their cages."

Noon originally started the Save the Chimps foundation back in 1997, when the U.S. Air Force—which had been leasing its flight-training chimps to research labs since the early 1970s—decided to get out of the chimp business altogether. Offering up its surplus inventory for bids, they awarded most of their chimps to Frederick Coulston, a native New Yorker who was among the first scientists in the country to perform toxicology and physiology experiments on primates in the 1940s. By the mid-1990s, Coulston, who died in 2003, had gone on to become the country's undisputed primate maven, owning more than six hundred chimpanzees, then roughly half the nation's total. Noon, with the support of Jane Goodall and other prominent primatologists, successfully sued the air force for custody of twenty-one of the chimps they had granted to Coulston, and then began raising money to start her Fort Pierce sanctuary to house them there.

After a series of Animal Welfare Act violations led to the deaths of dozens of Coulston's chimps and a loss of government funding, he filed for bankruptcy in 2002. Carole Noon, with the help of a $7 million grant from the Arcus Foundation, acquired the facility. She moved into a twenty-eight-foot-long house trailer at the rear of the grounds and, with the assistance of local contractors and Save the Chimps staff, immediately set about trying to soften and brighten the place's many dark, hard edges.

She spent $500,000 alone on remodeling the cages, expanding them outward and upward with overhead "penthouses," allowing the chimps their first views of the sky and of the nearby Sacramento Mountains. In the three years since Noon had taken over, she'd managed to upgrade "hell" to a kind of primate purgatory, where the remaining occupants were now awaiting deliverance to their future island paradise in Fort Pierce.

"So," Noon said, showing me through the entrance to Building 700, "ready to be horrified?"

Seated before me on the cement floor of a narrow, rank-smelling anteroom to Building 700's main chimp cell block were Dr. Jocelyn Bezner, the staff veterinarian, and the staff caregiver, Jen Feurstein, the two of them staring through the bars of a portable pen at a soundly sleeping Oliver. Bezner was holding one of Oliver's huge, black leathery fingers, jutting out between the bars. I slowly sidled up to the cage and—as I've been wanting to do so often here with Roger—grabbed another of the sleeping Oliver's fingers, gently squeezing it.

Through the pair of swinging doors just behind us, Oliver's pals had by now worked themselves up into a full-fledged frenzy. Noon opened one of the doors to say hello to everyone and try to settle things down a bit. Inside was a picture of true bedlam: opposing rows of cages, twelve deep, scores of chimps—many of them quite scrawny and scarred, with raw skin patches from having plucked out their own hair—swaying and dashing, whooping and screeching. A chimp named Devon seemed to be the maestro of the mayhem, grabbing hold of the bars of the cage nearest the door, madly thrusting himself forward and back, screaming.

Just then I felt Oliver's finger twitch slightly in my palm, and now he was sitting bolt upright, eyes wide. His mouth was fixed in a kind of hysterical grin that gradually expanded, as if he were trying to get more air, into a soundless, slow-motion version of a chimp's fright scream, finally culminating in a series of short, breathy, high-pitched squeals.

"It's okay, it's okay," Dr. Bezner kept repeating to him softly, and then once more to the rest of us. "He's just hallucinating."

After a few moments, Oliver tilted back over to sleep, despite all the racket around him. Noon signaled to me that we should be going, to let things simmer down. As we were headed toward the door, Dr. Bezner went over to Devon's cell and in a beautiful, clear soprano began bringing Devon and the rest of Building 700 back down to earth with the opening strains of the Irving Berlin standard "Cheek to Cheek" (Devon's favorite, for obvious reasons: "Heaven, I'm in heaven . . .").

Noon next led me over to a small cinder-block building in which Coulston's toxicology experiments were once conducted. Inside were two large, adjacent cages. One side of each cage could be squeezed inward on conveyors, making each cage the width of a chimpanzee if need be, to facilitate the injection of whatever drug or disease was being tested. As I was peering inside one of the cages, Noon shut the building door. The place went pitch dark.

"Okay," she said. "Your number's up. You're called in for research. If you're lucky you've got somebody next door for company. You've got a squeezable cage and you're getting some drug in ever-increasing doses to see what happens to you. And that's your life."

As we were leaving, Noon noticed me staring up at the only

other fixture in the room, what looked like one of those elevated, wall-mounted TV stands you see in hospital rooms.

"You got it," Noon said, walking off. "That was their enrichment. It's amazing they're not more maniacal than they are."

Our final stop of the day was Building 300, Coulston's former breeding compound, referred to now by Save the Chimp staff members simply as "the dungeon." It had a similar arrangement of long, opposing rows of adjacent cement and steel cages, enclosures that, before Noon's modest renovations, were only slightly larger than the minimum five feet by five feet by seven feet required, to this day, by federal law for the lifelong keeping of animals that get as big as Roger.

Noon had us wait by the swinging front doors to the main cell block of Building 300 so that staff members could get the chimps to their outside cells, thus clearing the way for our passing. The occupants, however, were proving to be somewhat uncooperative.

"Oh, no!" Noon shouted, scrunching up her shoulders and then calmly striding off, revealing the feces-splattered back of her blue denim work shirt. Plum, a female chimp in one of the first cages, had somehow managed to peg Noon through an opening in the front doors no wider than six inches.

Throwing feces, along with various forms of self-mutilation, is another common behavioral pathology of prolonged primate captivity, something I witnessed often while working some years ago as a creative writing teacher at the Ossining Correctional Facility, formerly Sing Sing Prison, up along the Hudson River in the town of Ossining, New York.

As Carole Noon went to a nearby staff laundry room to change her shirt, I looked through a small windowpane in one of the doors of Building 300.

A staff worker at the far back of the building was struggling forward, head down, arms flailing, Plum's successful strike having set off a feces-flinging and water-spitting maelstrom.

"They don't really enjoy that," Noon said to me as we were starting back toward Coulston's front office building. "Normal chimps will wipe their feet off when they step in it. But these chimps here? Well . . . when you start thinking this is fun, it suggests deep disturbances, and it's sick."

The following day I flew back to Houston and began the drive east along the northern shore of the Gulf of Mexico toward Florida, having made a promise to Noon that I'd come to see the "happy ending" to her chimps' saga: the two-hundred-acre patch of former orange groves in Fort Pierce that was now being carved into a series of thirteen three-acre, moated islands, each with attached housing units of private sleeping quarters and numerous skylights.

"Look at it," Noon said as we were hopping into her golf cart days later for my initial tour of the facility, "some of the prettiest real estate in Florida and guess who's moving in. Not rich people."

Only one of the islands, the original oasis to which Noon retired her first twenty-one air force chimps, was operational at that point, a huge, multiacre expanse of verdant knolls, jungle-gym platforms, suspended catwalks, and earthen culverts dotted with trees and shrubbery. Here and there I could see these black blobs, which, as Noon pulled up to one fenced-off corner of the island, suddenly began to move, gamboling toward us in nearly upright, front-fisted strides.

"Just for them to have that option of running," Noon said, gesturing at the approaching chimps. "That's what tickles me so much about this property."

I found it somewhat disconcerting at first to see the chimps in such a setting. It wasn't just the anomaly of chimpanzees freely swinging and striding against a backdrop of Florida orange groves. For me getting any glimpse into their actual nature only seemed to further distinguish them and diminish us. A diminishment accentuated, in this instance, by the fact that these chimps appeared to be so much larger than those back in Alamogordo, for the most part because they'd stopped the self-mutilation, and all had gotten their health and their hair back.

At one point a very large chimp named Waylan—a chimp quite similar in both size and disposition to Roger—muscled his way toward us.

"He's one of the largest chimps I've ever known," Noon said to me, Waylan coming right up to the fence before us and settling in alongside a female named Dana. "The largest and the sweetest. Waylan is very shy. Born in captivity. Didn't know how to be around other chimps. So when it was time to try to get Waylan to meet somebody, I said to myself, 'Who out of all these people can he meet?' And I thought, Dana. She's forty-two, born in Africa, and she's so socially sophisticated. So nice. So I open the door to let them meet. Waylan's afraid. Doesn't move. She climbs up and sits in the doorway. She looks at Waylan and literally takes his chin in her hand and lifts his face so he can look at her. That's Dana. She's the queen!"

Lunch hour for the Save the Chimp staff that day soon gave way to the chimps' midday feeding. We were all sitting around a picnic table in front of the compound's headquarters when Noon stood and clanged an old-fashioned ranch dinner bell hanging from a post just overhead. She waited a moment and then rang it again.

"That did it," she said. "Here they come."

Off in the distance, we could see the black blobs on the move again, row upon row of them, coming across the island's grassy mounds, past the strung catwalks and huge platform jungle gyms, toward the chimps' central housing quarters. Noon and I and some of the staff members started over to meet them. Once all the chimps had made their way inside, the feasting began, chunks of fresh cucumbers and carrots and oranges giving off, in stark contrast to Coulston, the strongest aromas in the place.

After lunch, Noon made sure all the doors leading back outside from the chimps' housing were secure so that we and staff members could clean up the island, much of it strewn with toys, baby dolls, plastic buckets, and wheel carts, like a vast kids' playground but one oddly infused with the wild's essence of danger. We were in their terrain now, on their footing.

From the center of the island, Noon pointed out to me the other soon-to-be-completed islands, each with its own pastel-hued housing unit, all the colors bright and upbeat—"everything as different from Coulston as possible," Noon explained. "No associations."

We started back across the island toward Save the Chimps headquarters, where Noon was to print up for me directions for getting here to the Center for Great Apes. As we were walking, Noon recalled for me a night back at Coulston when, just after the renovations to the old cages had been completed, the chimps were allowed to move into their outer enclosures and could see the dark desert sky for the first time. Until then, they had been locked inside every day by 4:00 P.M. Noon said that as she sat out on the steps of her house trailer that night at the back of Coulston's grounds, she could hear all of the buildings "talking to each other. Everyone was talking.

"I understood some of it," she said. "It was, Look at the stars, and look at the moon, and what do you think all of that is about? And how long do you think it is going to last? But then they started saying something different. Something I didn't understand. I struggled for the longest time to make sense of what it was. And here's what I think they were saying. They were announcing themselves to the night, to the world. They were saying, We live here, too. We exist."

Five fifteen A.M. Noises. Human, I think, coming from near the infirmary. A building door opening and closing. It's a little early for the morning shift.

Roger is still so awake. Wanting. Watchful. The slightest movement from me in the direction of packing up, and he'll be off in that corner again.

And yet I'm thinking now that our time is up regardless. That in the end I've only been hurting Roger by being with him like this. Forestalling his return to his true self by having aligned myself too closely with his disturbed one.

It was most likely never me that he recognized anyway, so much as all the kindred places I've just been, right down to that one encounter with wild chimpanzees that Roger himself has never had. As though, like some sort of simian shaman, he did feel through me the tendrils of what should have been his experience all along. Felt them even as I first stood out there by the front gate a week ago, staring in at the curved upper steel boughs and fruit-flecked palm fronds of this little Erector set forest.

There was Ragan's golf cart, and the diapered Knuckles now seated beside me as we started in, Ragan and I going from one enclosure to the next, greeting the others, and yes, I'm thinking, I remember Koda, who pulled down his pants and sat on the office copy machine; and Sammy from the big screen; and, of course, the trunk monkey chimps; and here now the wide-eyed Bam Bam, lolling about in the metal walkway above Ragan and me; Bam Bam, who faithfully threw around his dinner salad on cue and started chewing on the tablecloth for the smiling evangelicals.

We tell Bam Bam good-bye and then drive farther along, the golf cart stopping in a squall of Chipper's screaming and feet-pounding, Butch and Chipper setting off the rest of the retirees high in the caged branches above, and with them the memory, still so fresh in my mind, of their counterparts in the wilderness, whose phantom cries and fleet movements I had just been chasing through the Ugandan jungle.

There was the day I'd spent hiking in Kyambura Gorge, a deep, seven-mile-long canyon just below the very village the elephants had attacked years earlier, the gorge where I'd been told a large pod of wild chimps still lived. It was a long, slow, one-mile descent toward its steamy base, the tree boughs high above all bound up in hoary vines, clamoring birdcalls, and the rising, thought-subsuming roar of the Kyambura River below, like passing out of time altogether.

Following along the river's banks, just the split seed casings and hollowed-out nutshells of past chimpanzee meals were enough to have me tightroping felled logs over hippo-filled waters before the next far-off volley of screams was pulling me for hours, fruitlessly, in another direction, and all the while that distant voice in my head wondering, Why am I so ready to die for this? Why would this be such a good way to die? Just trying to see what Roger, my-as-yet unfound former primal self, never has and never will.

A full week later, in the Kibale rain forest, four hours north of Queen Elizabeth, my last day out in the bush, I found myself staring at the same torn-open fruit pods, and the makeshift spoons that the chimpanzees there had fashioned of fallen palm fronds.

My guide, Geoffrey, was pointing out to me a few abandoned chimp nests in the trees above when a sudden, distant drumming stopped us, and soon I was being signaled over by Geoffrey to the base of a tree called a "pepeteneto." It had huge, flying-buttress-like prop roots, the tautly stretched bark between which Geoffrey was now pounding with the base of his palms, the same way, he explained, that the Kibale's chimps do it, drumming out signals when one of them gets lost, or to play the loudest to establish dominance, or simply to make music.

We started in the direction of their drumbeats, and then, as though in complete befuddlement over the possible significance of Geoffrey's poundings, the drumming stopped.

A long time passed without another notable chimpanzee sound. Miles away by then from the Uganda Wildlife Authority outpost from which we'd departed that morning, Geoffrey checked his watch and said we had better turn around if we were to get back before dusk, taking our chances at crossing paths with some chimps on our return swing.

We'd get no more than a few steps when it came: one shrill scream, not unlike the one that first got things going here tonight and seemingly as close. Geoffrey took hold of my wrist a moment while he got the best fix on which way to go, and then after we'd run a good mile in that direction, a huge volley of screams and an attendant scramble through the underbrush would send us the other way.

Back and forth we went, the chimps' movements so swift it soon became apparent that any encounter with them was to be entirely on their terms: a group of chimps who had just decided to settle in somewhere and wait for us, or who were already so comfortably established in their treetop nests that they'd not mind a peek at these two mostly hairless, strangely upright beasts stumbling around through the brush below.

Before long, Geoffrey—half my age, a young, newly hired guide for the Uganda Wildlife Authority—was disappearing up ahead of me in hallucinatory wobbles of heat. Still, I refused to call out to him for fear of scaring off any nearby pod of chimps and ruining the very moment that I'd been madly chasing down, like some voracious predator of my own primordial past.

"Keep on . . ." the inner bog voice was telling me, and far through the thick brush and Kibale heat I could all at once see Geoffrey again.

He was standing stock-still, his right hand pointing straight up. My eyes didn't register his other hand until I'd drawn a bit closer to him: the base of Geoffrey's palm resting at his hip, his cupped fingers gently drawing me closer with those residual, slow-pulsing wing flaps of a just-landed butterfly.

I came up alongside him. Geoffrey squeezed my arm, only his eyes directing mine toward the cageless, sun-mottled canopy above.

"Congratulations," he said, and I'd think of that often afterward, the odd choice of words, as though a birth of some sort had just occurred; as though I'd somehow fathered a moment from my own remote ancestry. One as yet so unformed and set so high above me that I thought it at first something completely different, a briefly riled flock of birds that was just now settling in again, the ropey wing flaps and hovered landings gradually coalescing into this deeply familiar treetop tableau of dark, lolling heads and limbs: a scratched shoulder; a snatched piece of fruit; a cradled infant; and that one baby chimp's face poking out over the edge of its nest for a long look down at me.

My eyesight suddenly blanched, and my thoughts went all

adrift, not from the sunlight so much, or fatigue and thirst, as from the want of an even deeper memory; one I knew my mind contained and yet could build me no bridge toward having.

"And that's Butch . . ." I could now hear Ragan saying, Butch's "ta-da!" pose reigniting Chipper's cries, and then the next squall of screams across this Erector set forest, the mayhem seemingly being stirred around and around by Butch's absurdly upraised hand.

There was another squeeze of my arm, and I looked down into that wide, swimmy-eyed smile of Knuckles; all the other retirees still swirling and screaming around us when that first, loud hand clap sounded, like a judge's gavel in a courtroom at last ungovernable, followed by two more, and I turned and saw for the first time my oldest friend: the man who, in the end, can find no bridge to being one.

Epilogue

I would delay leaving Roger for as long as I could that morning, only minutes in the end, but plenty long enough, it seems now, for the both of us.

"Five nineteen A.M.," was the time of my last notebook entry. Those noises I'd been hearing from the direction of the infirmary had briefly abated. Still with the rapidly diminishing darkness, the thought of having to pack up and flee before being detected was soon inciting the attendant worry that Roger would, at any moment, detect my distraction and desert me. One way or another, our time was clearly up, and the urge to reach out to him, whatever the consequences, had now become too strong.

It was all I could do at first to maintain my focus, to ward off all skittishness, suppress the resurgence of my long-dormant spindle cells and keep on abiding the apparent blankness. But drawing upon a week of speechless stares, and felt silences, and osmotic inference, I soon gave myself back over to Roger's gaze, hearing only that inner, far-off voice again, calling me onward; urging my hand once more through the air beyond that painted red line.

Roger watched it with wild intent, as though espying through thick brush some rare shorebird being lifted will-lessly toward him by sudden wind gusts in soft parenthetical flights along the sand.

And all at once we weren't there at all, but back in that not so distant time when he and I were, in fact, one and the same. I imagined Roger holding perfectly still as my hand finally alighted, squeezing first the cracked casement of his forefinger and then pulling me even closer to him, up over the knuckle, my entire hand only coming fully to rest, feeling the truest calm, upon the warm, open expanse of the back of his.

It was, in the end, such a brief distance to go to find Roger. No longer than that first foray his ancestors never took with ours.

How to describe it?

Out along the field path I walk each summer between the cabin and my work shed there is one spot, a slight concavity in the earth with a vortical whorl of hay in it, like those tight, pin-wheeled swirls of hair (are they origin or end points?) that you see on the back of a human head, or on the haunches of a dog, and that I even saw early one morning up at the cabin in the fur around the eye of a moose.

I was lying awake in the downstairs cabin bed, near dawn, reading beside a soundly sleeping Bex and our pint-sized terrier mix, Roz, the birds only beginning to unwind their heads into the gathering light.

I noticed at one point a shadow at the corner of my book's right-hand page. There was this sudden enormous breathing, like that of a newly formed planet, and then my entire book was eclipsed, and turning toward the bedside window, my eyes were now little ice moons in the thrall of a huge, glassy brown orb.

It held there for so long that I soon found myself noticing those same pinwheel hair swirls in the fur around the moose's eye and all along its massive dark brown skull and jaw, all of them whirling and bursting forth like some medieval tapestry of the firmament.

The very first impulse of matter, I think—just after it had decoupled from light and the universe was born—must have been in this same whirling motion, so prevalent is it in all of life's subsequent, spun-out forms, from the Earth's very core right up to its surface field grasses and the winds that comb them: an entire universe of miniomphali, each of them echoing the original.

Animals, of course, are far more attuned to these universal "sweet spots"—apparent vacuities that are, in fact, little trapdoors to infinity. I, in truth, would probably never have noticed the one along the field path if not for Roz. Whenever she follows me out to the work shed, or when we're walking back to the cabin together, she can't keep herself from doing a full-scale, seemingly boneless collapse into that one spot, holding there, pressing herself into it long after I've passed on by, as though trying to meld again with the elemental nonher.

And yet it was some semblance of those body-long field dives of Roz's that I felt with Roger that morning: one final, deep, earthward tug, and easeful, off of that illusory plane of my separateness, my expulsion, from him and from the rest of creatures. As though I had somehow pushed or fallen through to the far side of that field path's sweet spot. As though I had, in fact, been taken by Roger. Been taken by him whole, and alive, and peacefully in.

I sat there staring at my hand, and then I looked up at him, only his eyelids moving, slowly closing and lifting again. I'd have thought him sleepy if I didn't know Roger. Sleepiness, in fact, was a prospect so unlike him and his hypervigilance that I began to interpret the droopy eyes as some sort of simian semaphore code, the slow, pensive slide of Roger's lids only heightening that sense of him as my confessor; each drifty blink a kind of "there, there, my son" assent to the sudden stream of apologies and avowed atonements that those very eyelid droops of his were now drawing from me.

I would do my utmost, I soon found myself promising Roger, to convey to others the substance of our extraordinary days together in the woods of Wauchula, Florida, and of our final night. To make known the contents of the black notebook, pages that I told him might ultimately constitute a kind of missive or manifesto on his behalf and that of all his fellow captives. Not just those in the world's growing number of Erector set forests but also, increasingly now, the inhabitants of the still-unbridled branches.

"The Wauchula Woods Accord," I think I said it might be called, the central premise being that the degree to which we humans will finally stop abusing other creatures and, for that matter, one another will ultimately be measured by the degree to which we come to understand how integral a part of us all other creatures actually are.

I carried on in this way for some time, but it wasn't long before I started hearing more noises again from the area of the infirmary. I felt my hand shift slightly, and then Roger was standing, looming once more above me. I promptly stood to keep at eye level with him, knocking my chair back. Outside, the noises grew louder. Chipper stirred in his blankets, and then Butch.

Strewn on the floor at my feet were my copy of *The Metaphysics of Apes* and some pens and minicassette tapes that had spilled from my satchel. I bent over to pick them up and then placed my folding chair against the opposite wall, exactly where I found it, Roger all the while patiently waiting by the front bars, watching me.

I came back, looked him once more in the eyes. Then I turned and left, stealing another peek at him from the areaway door: the backs of Roger's legs going away, and the palms of his hands dangling down beside his calves.

He went silently past the pile of magazines and Yellow Pages in the middle of his room and, the last I saw of him, was not making for his back-wall sulking place, but toward his corner-mounted platform bed, swinging as swiftly and soundlessly upward as when he'd originally swept down.

He is up there at his usual spot by that bedside window, I remember fondly thinking as I passed through the outer areaway and started off in the direction of the cottage. He's up there not to manically rock his way through another sunrise, but just for a quick look at me, his other half, before at last turning over for some much-needed sleep.

I walked on contentedly, past the other retirees' places, everyone still sleeping soundly. And then, just as I was reaching the cottage's front door, a series of high-pitched pant-hoots emanated from the direction of Roger's place, instantly setting off the next compoundwide conflagration of screams and pounding.

I slipped back inside the cottage, went out once more to the back porch, the first daylight gathering now at the forest's edge, and sat there beneath the slow-whirling ceiling fan, listening to the ongoing ruckus.

It would be a good hour before the place settled down again, me waiting all the while for a knock at the cottage's front door: Ragan or one of the caregivers, having espied me making my way back to the cottage, wanting to know what had happened. What had I done?

The image of a deeply riled, inconsolable Roger was etched now in my brain, and my worst fear confirmed, because I believed I had, with my own hand, reawakened Roger to his. Had become, in essence, his troubled history's dreaded white-haired man.

I don't recall when I finally crawled into bed that morning. I caught a few hours' sleep, then got up and began packing my things for good, leaving the Center for Great Apes at about noon that same day without saying any last good-byes. I told myself that if Roger was the one who'd let out those screams, I was the last person he should see again. If he wasn't, if things were truly settled between us, then I'd rather have our last departure that morning be the one by which we remembered each other.

I did go over to Ragan's house to tell her I was going, that something had come up at home that I needed to tend to, but I found her place dark and the front door locked. Over at the office compound, an assistant told me that Patti had left very early that morning to catch a flight to visit relatives on the West Coast, something I only then remembered her having mentioned to me earlier in the week.

I went back and left Ragan a thank-you note out on the porch. I then grabbed my bags and headed toward the side delivery gate behind the cottage, where I had been instructed to leave my car the day I arrived. The compound seemed to me strangely quiet as I left, and I couldn't help wondering if that dreaded ennui that pervades human Sundays also afflicted our nearest kin.

It would be a few weeks before I finally called the Center for Great Apes to speak with Ragan, unable to get from my mind the thought of Roger and of that last morning's ghostly swell of screams.

Ragan was, of course, out on the grounds somewhere. She'd have to be paged. Would I mind holding?

A good five minutes passed. This struck me as ominous, an indication that I was on the cusp of a conversation Ragan had been both anticipating and saving some spleen for. Otherwise, why not just say she'd call me back at a less busy point?

"Well, Charles," her familiar voice finally intoned and with the usual busy breathiness. "I don't know what happened exactly, but I have to tell you . . ."

Lawsuit was the first thought that came to mind and with it the image once more of that esteemed rat defender Bartholomew Chassenee, striding back and forth before a packed courtroom and a wild-eyed, teeth-rubbing Roger seated on the witness stand, Chassenee wielding the latest MRI images of Roger's brain and of all the spindle cells I had either broken or permanently stunted in the course of our days together and of that one last, illicit night.

"It's simply amazing to me," I could hear Ragan saying now. "He's an entirely different chimp."

She went on to describe how in the days after my departure, in the course of another series of socialization experiments, Roger had now been not only amenable to such interactions but also the most willing and able arbiter of them, eagerly embracing his fellow retirees, even settling disputes among them and initiating play. He had, I was told, become particularly close buddies with, of all chimps, Chipper.

"Just today," Ragan said, "Roger and Chipper were tickling and laughing, chasing, grooming, hugging, holding hands, holding feet, bumping heads and laughing more. It brought us all to tears."

It was, Ragan said, a change that some of the caregivers had begun to detect in Roger the very day I left. They had, it seems, run out very early that morning in the midst of a great uproar, eventually tracing the core commotion to Roger's place, where, rushing in through the open areaway doors, they found Butch and Chipper in a scuffle.

But throughout all the commotion Roger was up in his bed, sound asleep, finally catching up on all those lost hours. He was still asleep, I was told, long past midday, and was later seen by some of the caregivers just hanging out on his bed, rolling around on his back, playing with his blanket, holding both feet in the air.

"Anyway," Ragan said with a sigh, "you wouldn't recognize him," and I remember feeling this sudden pang, my immediate, selfish worry being, does this mean that Roger would no longer recognize me?

"And what about you?" Ragan asked now, as though she'd been reading my thoughts. "Did you ever figure out what this thing was between you and him?"

I told her I wasn't sure. That just about the only definitive thing I'd been able to deduce from our time together was that Roger and I couldn't possibly have met before. That I had scoured the years since Roger's birth for any meetings with a captive chimpanzee, and that none of the ones I'd come up with could have involved him.

Ragan listened patiently to my odd little trilogy of chimp encounters from that summer of '79. And then somewhere in the midst of my recounting of that last Lower East Side, Airstream interlude, the phone went strangely silent.

"You didn't happen to notice if that vehicle had Connecticut license plates, did you?"

"I have no idea," I said. "Why?"

"Oh, nothing. It's just that Roger's original owners were a family from Connecticut. They're the ones that sold him when he wasn't even two to the circus trainer in Florida."

The rest of the story, the one I've since chosen to believe, is, by now, all perfectly formed in my mind, but I knew even then, even with Patty Ragan holding there at the other end of the line, that I wasn't about to let anything, certainly not the intervention of a new and potentially contradictory fact—something so limiting, for example, as the truth (whatever that is, exactly)—alter my story's outcome.

I could see now, clearly, the baby Roger stepping out onto to the sidewalk that late August morning before my East Third Street stoop, shading his brow, looking briefly up and down the block before locking eyes with mine. Could see, in perfect miniature, Roger's tiny freckled face and his mouthful of as yet unabraded teeth.

The remaining details—the ones that have since come back to me in the course of that natural fleshing out of the ill-remembered past that we with the added spindle cells call "history"—all fit perfectly into place now as well: the construction crew just up the block, digging out and setting off to one side—in neat little air-piling motions—the layers of old city street; and baby Roger's upraised hand, held there for the taking as neighbors approached from one direction and from the other, Mike the Bike—big and broad-shouldered, his bleached-white hair catching menacing glints of sunlight. I stared once more at Roger then turned and rushed away from him, only to look down moments later from my upstairs apartment at a lone, side-walk-stranded chimp, staring up at a rising facade of sun-flecked city windows, trying to find again somewhere among them his first and oldest friend.

"I don't know who the family is," Ragan was saying now, "but I suppose we could try to find out in case you want to get ahold of them."

"Well," I said, pretending to consider this for a moment, "we could, but what would be the point?"

She laughed and then told me I was welcome to return and see Roger whenever I wanted.

Roger, if I am to be true to myself now and to him, was the one who made the first gesture toward leaving that last morning together at the Center for Great Apes, pulling his hand away from the front crossbar of his bedroom. He was sensing, I think, my need to get out of there. Was giving me leave to go.

He stood by, as I say, while I rushed about putting my notebook and pens away in my shoulder satchel, and *The Metaphysics of Apes* and my minicassettes, and then grabbed the folding chair and put it back against the wall opposite Roger's bedroom door.

It wasn't until I returned and stood briefly before him again that I realized how tired, in fact, Roger was—gentle, sleepy man—only those slow-drifting lids of his betraying his true drowsiness. Still, he waited, as usual, for me to turn away first before he started to leave, doing his quick, soundless, three-point shuffle off through the strewn Yellow Pages and magazines at the center of his room, then going straight up, with one swift, smooth swing, into his blanket-nested corner bed.

He was, I am certain of it now, watching out that little bedside window of his when I left, waiting for me to reappear on the other side of the areaway, and then watching my figure recede toward the cottage, the very fact of my going away at last not upsetting or disappointing him.

He didn't go directly to sleep, I think, but lay there on his back for a bit, the way the caregivers would later see him do, holding on to his upraised feet, just like a child—the one I never had, and the one that Roger reminded me I still am.

He lolled about up there on his back for some time, playing with his blanket, lost in a reverie, Roger announcing in his own way, and in a place where there are, at last, no more of our words: I live here, too. I exist.

Acknowledgments

First and foremost I'd like to thank Patti Ragan both for the work she does on behalf of captive apes and for her great generosity in allowing me the extraordinary access that made this book possible. My days with Roger and with Ragan's other charges at the Center for Great Apes in the woods of Wauchula will stay with me always. Those wishing to express gratitude for her efforts in the form of much-needed donations can learn how to do so by going to www.centerforgreatapes.org.

Many thanks go out as well to the other lady liberators and defenders of captive chimpanzees I met in the course of my journey: Linda Koebner and Linda Brent at Chimp Haven; Carole Noon at the Save the Chimps foundation; and to Theo Capaldo at the New England Anti-Vivisection Society for her tireless efforts on behalf of chimpanzees and other animals currently being abused in research.

The travels that inform this book took me well beyond the story of chimpanzees. The people whose experiences and expertise I've borrowed from are therefore too numerous to name. I would, however, like to express my gratitude to Sam Gosling of the Animal Personality Institute at the University of Texas, Austin; to the great Eve Abe, for her courage and compassion in the ongoing fight to help Uganda's equally beleaguered human and elephant populations; and to Gay Bradshaw, a true trailblazer on this fraught frontier between humans and other animals and a trusted confidant in my less sure moments about how to negotiate that illusory boundary in language.

To Rick Schlueter and to Connie and Mike Casey I am grateful for admitting me into their lives on such short notice.

Thanks to Raymond Corbey of Tilburg University and Leiden University in the Netherlands for his compelling book *The Metaphysics of Apes,* which was to become both a physical and a spiritual presence over the course of my days with Roger and the other apes.

To Jeffrey Greene and Susan Prospere I am ever grateful, as I am to James Ryerson, for helping me first get my head and words around many of the subjects and ideas in this book; to Gerry Marzorati, a great friend and mind; to Jon Lee and Erica Anderson, for the wonderful weeks at their home in Dorset where this book was completed; and to Francisco Goldman, John Tintori, and Mary Cybulski.

At Scribner, thank you to Jessica Manners for all her help and to my editor, Colin Harrison, for his well-tuned vigilance and gentle persistence. This was our first book together and I hope not the last.

Chuck Verrill has been so supportive on all fronts for so long that none of my books could have happened without him. There's no way to adequately express my thanks.

To my family, an ongoing source of solace and support, thank you.

Finally, I wish to thank from the very bottom of my heart Neal Epstein and his wife, Debbie, for the use of their lovely cottage in the Blue Ridge Mountains, and for nothing less than saving my heart when a sudden illness struck this past year. To you and the folks at the National Institutes of Health, Dr. Douglas Rosing, Brenda Holbrook, and Dr. Neal Babar among them, I literally owe my life.

About the Author

Charles Siebert is the author of *Wickerby: An Urban Pastoral,* a *New York Times* Notable Book of 1998; *A Man After His Own Heart*; and the novel *Angus*. His essays, articles, and poems have appeared in numerous publications including *The New York Times Magazine, The New Yorker, Harper's, Esquire, Vanity Fair, Outside,* and *Men's Journal.* He lives with his wife in Brooklyn, New York.

Printed in the United States
By Bookmasters